The Philosophy of Art of Karl Marx

The Philosophy of Art of

Karl Marx

Mikhail Lifshitz

Translated from the Russian by Ralph B Winn

 Pluto Press Limited

First published in Russian 1933

This translation first published 1938 by
the Critics Group, New York

Republished 1973 by Pluto Press
All rights reserved

ISBN paperback 0 902818 34 1
ISBN hardback 0 902818 35 X

Designed by Lone Morton

Pluto Press Ltd,
Unit 10 Spencer Court,
7 Chalcot Road,
London NW1 8LH

Printed in Great Britain by
Bristol Typesetting Co. Ltd., Barton Manor, St. Philips
Bristol

Publisher's note

This translation was first published in 1938 by the New York Critics Group as no. 7 in the Critics Group Series, edited by Angel Flores. All footnotes except nos 28-36 and nos 38 and 68 were added by him. These, we assume, were in the original Russian edition. We have brought all other footnotes up to date, referring to the most accessible English editions and translations of Marx's (and Engels') works where appropriate and have corrected a number of mistakes which crept into the footnotes of the 1938 edition. The text itself has not been altered.

We would like to thank Terry Eagleton for providing us with a short preface for this edition.

Preface

Given the fact that Karl Marx had more urgent tasks on his hands than the formulation of a systematic aesthetic theory, the title of this book might appear to claim too much. That the title isn't in fact unjustified is clear enough once the wide terrain on which it allows Lifshitz to enter is fully recognised. There have been other studies of Marx's writings on art and literature, but few of them have been concerned, as this book is, to analyse Marx's aesthetic judgements as an element within his general theoretical development. Lifshitz refuses to *abstract* a 'philosophy of art' from the corpus of Marx's writings, as bourgeois literary criticism has commonly done; instead he sets out to trace some crucial aesthetic themes in Marx's work in terms of their integral relations to the developing totality of his thought.

In doing so, Lifshitz implicitly undermines the case that the scattered, often fragmented nature of Marx's comments on art and literature reflects a merely casual, empirical, intermittent interest in the subject on Marx's part, and that this is the sinister consequence of 'putting economics first'. On the contrary, he demonstrates how, from his own early experiments in a variety of literary forms right through to the aesthetic implications of some of the categories used in *Capital*, Marx had a close and continuous engagement in imaginative production. It was an engagement which, as Lifshitz shows, is active within a whole range of Marx's theoretical positions. The issue of art is a controversial one in his early relations with Hegel and the Young Hegelians; it enters into his analysis of ancient societies and the ideological function of religion; in the form of an onslaught on Romanticism, it enters into his critique of the reactionary politics of the German ruling class. Far from being a mere side-interest or embellishment, it appears as a subordinate but significant factor in Marx's understanding of social production, the division of labour and the product as commodity; its influence can be traced in the development of the concepts of fetishism, sensuousness and abstraction.

It is for this reason that Lifshitz refuses to restrict himself to the more familiar topics of Marx's aesthetics. His analysis stretches to Marx's doctoral thesis on Epicurus as well as to the discussion of Greek art in the *Grundrisse*, to *Capital* as well as to the literary arguments of *The Holy Family*. 'Philosophy of art', then, suggests less a specialised sub-section of Marx's writings than a coherent and original standpoint from which to survey part of the trajectory of his work. But this isn't to say, on the other hand, that the topic is chosen for merely methodological reasons, any more than Marx's own interest in art and literature was merely methodological. The situation is more complex than that. Art can only be studied historically, and yet like all superstructures has its relative autonomy; it is powerless by itself to emancipate men struggling within class-society, and yet, even within the present, can provide powerful images of such emancipation. In the *Economic and Philosophical Manuscripts,* Marx seems to see in art a prefiguring of the refined and intensified senses of men liberated from historical alienation; but he insists too that only by an objective development of human nature will such a 'wealth of subjective *human* sensuality' be released. The final sentence of this book, which calls 'Art is dead!' and then adds 'Long live art!' seems true to this insight.

The Philosophy of Art of Karl Marx

Karl Marx, the greatest thinker and leader of the revolutionary working-class movement, was born at a time when men's interests had already begun to turn from literature and art to political economy and sociology.

Even the eighteenth century, that classic age of aesthetics, could not remain confined to abstractions such as 'the beautiful' and 'the sublime'. In the background of purely aesthetic discussions concerning the role of genius, the value of art, the imitation of nature, practical problems of the bourgeois-democratic movement intruded themselves with increasing insistence.

The great French Revolution marked a transition in this respect. The 'aesthetic period' in the development of the third estate ended at that point where the interests of the bourgeoisie were severed from the interests of society as a whole. In the course of time, the attitude of the bourgeoisie towards art became frankly practical. Problems of art were everywhere bound up with problems of business and politics; the quest for aesthetic freedom was followed by the struggle for laissez-faire and protective tariffs. And once the bourgeoisie attained political dominance, problems of history and art lost all public significance, and became the property of a narrow circle of scholars.

It was at this time that the independent revolutionary movement of the proletariat began. The working class was not concerned about the shift of social interest from poetry to prose. Quite the contrary, the sooner the 'beautiful' revolution could be succeeded by an 'ugly' one (as Marx liked to put it), the sooner the surface glamour of democratic illusions could be stripped from material interests to reveal the open class struggle, the nearer the ultimate goal of the proletarian movement. The founders of Marxism sought the secret of the exploitation of the working class in the economy of bourgeois society; and it was in the conquest of political power, in the dictatorship of the proletariat, that they found the means of its emancipation. Thus the doctrine of the historical role of the proletariat as the grave-diggers of capitalism and the creators of socialist society became the *distinguishing feature* of Marx's outlook, the *basic content* of which was, of course, his economic theory. The 'aesthetic period' ended with Goethe and Hegel.

Whatever the views of the founders of Marxism concerning artistic creation, they could not deal with it as extensively as the philosophers of the preceding period had traditionally done. In a sense it is no doubt to be regretted that Marx and Engels left no systematic interpretation of culture and art. However, their failure to do so only proves that the founders of international working-class solidarity were fully equal to their historical task, and concentrated all their thought and effort upon the fundamental problem of suffering and struggling humanity. The revolutionary problem of Marx and Engels consisted in finding a means of breaking away from purely ideological criticism of the social order, and in discovering the everyday causes of all manifestations of man's activities.

In dealing with questions of art and culture, the importance of Marxist theory would be immense even if nothing were known about the aesthetic views of the founders of Marxism. Fortunately, however, this is not the case. In their works and correspondence there are many remarks and entire passages expressing their ideas on various phases of art and culture. As aphorisms, they are profound and significant, but, like all aphorisms, they admit of somewhat arbitrary interpretation.

It is at this point that the work of the scholar begins. He must connect these remarks with the general development of Marxism. Marx's aesthetic views are integrally bound up with his revolutionary world outlook. They have more than a mere biographical significance, although for various reasons we possess only fragments of his thoughts on art. In this connection the earliest sources belong to that period of his political development which might be called the period of revolutionary democratism.

1

Aesthetic problems occupied a conspicuous place in Marx's early intellectual life. In his university days (1835-41) he studied in addition to law and philosophy, the history of literature—chiefly ancient literature—as well as the classical German aestheticians. At the University of Bonn, which he entered in the autumn of 1835 as a student of criminal law, Marx devoted as much attention to the history of art and literature as to jurisprudence. He attended Schlegel's lectures on ancient literature; he delved into ancient mythology, a subject lectured upon at that time by the famous Welcker; he studied modern art. At the University of Berlin, Marx attended only one course in the history of literature (Geppert's lectures on Euripides, 1840-41), but his independent work in connection with creative art is of particular interest to us: among the books which he read in 1837 were Lessing's *Laocoön*, Winckelmann's *History of Ancient Art* and Reimarus' *Allgemeine Betrachtungen über die Trieben der Thiere*. In the course of his transition to Hegelianism, Marx made a thorough study of Hegel's *Aesthetik*, read, no doubt, during the summer of 1837.

Young Marx's interest in art was not confined to theory, however. He made numerous attempts to write verse, which, with some exceptions, were not particularly successful. In Bonn he wrote a philosophical poem which he sent his father (1835). To his Berlin period belong whole exercise books of verse dedicated to his fiancée, as well as forty other poems, the first act of a dramatic fantasy,

Oulanem, and several chapters of a humorous sketch, *Scorpion und Felix,*[1] written in the style of Sterne and Hoffmann.

As he himself confessed, Marx made determined efforts to suppress his inclination to write poetry; the temptation remained with him, however, for many years. As late as 1841 he published two of his early poems in *Athenäum.*[2] The conflict between the urge to write poetry and the stern necessity of finding an answer in the field of science to the problems of life constituted the first crisis in Marx's intellectual development.

The outcome of this inner battle was a complete renunciation of poetry and a conversion to the philosophy of Hegel, with its doctrine of the inevitable decadence of art in modern times.

Twice before in the history of German social thought there had been grave doubts as to the possibility of genuine artistic creativity under the new bourgeois relations. Shortly before the French Revolution classical German philosophy had given expression to aesthetic criticism of reality, and similar motives reappear in the thirties and forties, in the radical-democratic movement culminating in Marx.

A society based upon the blind struggle of egoistic interests, a society whose development is subject solely to the mechanical 'pressure of wants'—this 'realm of necessity' as Schiller called it—cannot serve as the soil for genuine artistic productivity. Such was the opinion of radical German youth at the time when Hegel and his fellow-students from Tübingen cultivated their so-called 'tree of freedom'. Their negative evaluation of actuality implied a criticism of the feudal world of privilege and the bourgeois domain of private property. In modern times, wrote young Hegel, folk poetry knows neither Harmodius nor Aristogeithon, 'whose fame will be eternal because they slew the tyrants and gave their fellow citizens equal

[1] Marx's poetry is available in the *Marx-Engels Gesamtausgabe* (MEGA), (Berlin 1927-), Abteilung I, Band I/2
[2] *Der Spielmann and Nachtliebe,* MEGA, I, I/1, p147

rights and equal laws'. Hegel contrasted the epoch of decline with the era of the ancient city-state, when 'the iron bond of necessity was still garlanded with roses', and the petty prosaic soul of private interest did not stifle the love of poetry and the appreciation of beauty. The paralyzing effects of the division of labour, the increasing mechanization of all forms of human activity, the engulfing of quality in quantity—all these typical characteristics of bourgeois society, Hegel recognized as inimical to poetry, even after he acknowledged capitalism to be the essential foundation of progress.

The 'day-dreaming terrorists' of the French Revolution (as Marx described the Jacobins) revolted against bourgeois economy not in order to abolish it, but rather in order to subordinate the material world of property to the political life of the citizens. The 'day-dreaming' element in the viewpoint of the eighteenth-century revolutionaries consisted precisely in this idealization of the political upper crust of society, in complete disregard of its sordid material basis. And similarly the great German idealists, even where they were critical of bourgeois society, spoke merely of the baseness of the sphere of economics in general, its inferiority to matters of the spirit. Only an abstract-spiritual solution of social contradictions is possible within the framework of idealist philosophy. Schiller (and the Romanticists) emphasized the aesthetic transcending of the 'realm of necessity': art, being an organ of the Absolute, should integrate that which history had divided, distorted and made antithetical. Hegel, on the other hand, considered *knowledge* the supreme weapon in the solution of existing contradictions; his last word is a stoical reconciliation with reality, a refusal to embellish it with artificial roses.

Thus Hegel, despite his many vacillations, was definitely pessimistic as to the possibility of artistic creation in modern times.

In the first period of his independent spiritual life, Marx was completely dominated by romanticism, and his attitude toward Hegel was decidedly negative. His romanticism, however, was of a radical, Fichtean hue. 'Onslaughts on the present' alternated with poetic appeals to the 'dignity of man', who continually forges ahead and overcomes the obstacles in his path. We find him a dreamer-enthusiast (the poem *Sehnsucht*), an iconoclast (*Des Verzweiflenden Gebet*), and in general a man determined to war against the eternal powers.

> *Und ihr schwindelt nicht vor Stegen,*
> *Wo der Gottgedanke geht,*
> *Wagt ihn an der Brust zu pflegen,*
> *Eig'ne Grösse ist Hochgebet.*[3]

Man may perish in this unequal combat, yet even his defeat is a triumph of the human spirit:

> *Und ihr Fallen selbst ist Siegen.*[4]

Despising Hegel for his refusal to struggle against reality, Marx ridiculed him as a 'pygmy', and poked fun at his *Aesthetik*:

> *Verzeiht uns Epigrammendingen,*
> *Wenn wir fatale Weisen singen,*
> *Wir haben uns nach Hegel einstudiert,*
> *Auf sein' Aesthetik noch nicht—abgeführt.*[5]

Marx himself described his poetry as 'idealistic' in the sense that it was dominated by the Fichtean contrast

---

[3] *Menschenstolz,* MEGA, I, I/2, p50
Nor do we become giddy in paths
Where the thought of God emanates;
We dare to cherish it in our breast.
Our own greatness is the highest prayer.

[4] *ibid*
And defeat itself is victory.

[5] *Epigramme,* in *ibid,* p42
Forgive us our epigrams
As we sing unpleasant tunes
For by rote we have studied Hegel,
And we are not yet purged of his *Aesthetic.*

between 'what is' and 'what ought to be'.[6] In one of his poems he likens 'what is' to a 'monkey's theatre', and he satirizes two pompous representatives of the bourgeois age —mathematicians, who reduce man's emotions to mathematical formulae, and physicians, who examine the world as if it were a bag of bones, and who consider the stomach the seat of all fantasy. The cure-all for vulgarity, suffering and triteness is poetry:

> Kühn gehüllt in weiten Glutgewanden,
> Lichtverklärt das stolzgehob'ne Herz,
> Herrschend losgesagt von Zwan und Banden,
> Tret'ich festen Schritt's durch weite Räume,
> Schmett're vor Dein Antlitz hin den Schmerz,
> Und zum Lebensbaum entsprühn die Träume![7]

In another poem this is even more clearly expressed:

> Wohl Sänger, weigt mich Blütentraum,
> Doch fass'ich auch in Himmelssaum,
> Und bind'in gold'nen Sternen;
> Es klingt das Spiel, das Leben weint,
> Das Spiel klingt fort, die Sonne scheint,
> Es sprühn in eins die Fernen.[8]

[6] Marx, letter to his father, 10 November 1837, in Loyd D Easton and Kurt H Guddat (eds), *Writings of the Young Marx on Philosophy and Society*, Anchor Books, New York, 1967 pp41-42

[7] *Schluss-Sonett an Jenny*, MEGA, I, I/2, p25
In ample glowing raiment bravely wrapped,
With pride-lifted heart illumined,
Constraints and ties imperiously renounced,
With firm step great spaces I traverse,
In thy presence I shatter pain,
Towards the tree of life my dreams radiate!

[8] *Wechselgespräch an . . .*, ibid, p38
O Bard, in flowered dreams I am enfolded,
But still I clasp the fringe of heaven,
To golden stars enfastened;
The play rings forth, life weeps,
And still the play rings forth, life weeps,
The distances radiate into one.

Here there is a transition to purely Schillerian motives. Somewhere there is a land where everyone is happy, where life and joy are one:

> *Bruderkuss und Herzenseinung*
> *Schliesset alle in den Kreis,*
> *Nicht mehr trennen Stand und Meinung,*
> *Leibe herrscht und ihr Geheiss.*[9]

But alas! this realm of happiness exists only in dreams:

> *Doch, 's ist nur ein nichtig Träumen,*
> *Das das warme Herz umfängt,*
> *Das aus Staub und Erdenräumen*
> *Sich zum Äther wogend drängt.*[10]

The gods, envious of man, make certain that he does not rise above natural necessity. Only in poetic fantasy is man free and happy. This conclusion, not unlike Schiller's

> *Was unsterblich im Gesang soll leben,*
> *Muss im Leben untergehn*[11]

expresses some degree of reunuciation from Fichtean romanticism. In his last poems Marx already revealed himself as reconciled to life. 'These last poems', he wrote to his father, 'are the only ones in which suddenly, as if at the stroke of a magic wand (the experience was, to begin

[9] *Lucinde, ibid,* p32
Brotherly kiss and unity of heart,
Bind all men within one circle,
No longer do rank and opinion cleave,
Love and its command prevail.

[10] *ibid*
Still it is only a futile dream
That the warm heart embraces
That out of the dust and earthly confines
Into the regions ethereal soars.

[11] *Die Götter Griechenlands, in Schillers Sämtliche Werke,* I, Stuttgart 1862, p68
Ah, that which gains immortal life in song,
To mortal life must perish!

with, overwhelming), the realm of true poetry opened up before me like a distant fairy palace, and then all my creations fell away to nothing.'[12]

In the summer of 1837 Marx's outlook underwent a profound change. He became dissatisfied with an abstract opposition between subject and object. 'Setting out from idealism (which, let me say in passing, I had compared to and nourished with that of Kant and that of Fichte), I proceeded to seek for the idea in the real itself. If hitherto the gods had soared above the earth, now they became its centre.'[13] The transition to Hegel was the result of an attempt to combine 'what is' and 'what ought to be', prose and poetry, after the manner of Goethe and young Schelling. 'I wrote a dialogue of some twenty-four pages: "Kleanthes, oder vom Ausgangspunkt und notwendigen Fortgang der Philosophie" [Cleanthes, or the Starting-Point and Necessary Progress of Philosophy]. Here, somehow, art and science, which had been wholly severed, were reunited.'[14] This work, for which Marx prepared himself with the aid of natural science, Schelling, and history, came to an unexpected conclusion. Originally planned to be in Schelling's vein, it turned out to be a statement of the Hegelian system. 'This work . . . this darling child of mine, reared in moonlight, lures me, like a false-hearted siren, into the clutches of the enemy,' wrote Marx.[15] And indeed from that moment on he bade farewell to the 'moonlight' of romanticism, and became a disciple of Hegel. Having met a group of young Hegelians, Marx planned, in fact, to publish a magazine to which many celebrities of the Hegelian school promised to contribute.

Marx's protests about the prosaic nature of reality, as expressed in his youthful poetry, constituted merely his first vague criticism of German 'feudalism turned bour-

---

[12] Marx, letter to his father, 10 November 1837, *op cit* (footnote 6), p46
[13] *ibid*
[14] *ibid*, p47
[15] *ibid*

geois'. Nor did he become conservative upon comprehending the secret of the Hegelian reconciliation with actuality; quite the contrary, his renunciation of romanticism signified a transition from a nebulous opposition to the existing order towards an even more radical criticism of social relations.

Because he portrayed the economic relations of bourgeois society with purely scientific detachment, the banker, Ricardo was accused of revolutionary motives. On the other hand he was also accused of heartless indifference to the suffering propertyless classes, and of compromising with social injustice. Something of the same sort happened to Hegel.

Hegel's aesthetics bore to the romantic philosophy of art the same relationship that Ricardo's pessimism bore to the sentimental utopias of the romantic economists. Before Marx, no economic theory had given to socialist thought such a mighty instrument of criticism of bourgeois society as the heartless 'cynicism' of Ricardo. Similarly, no work of classical German aesthetic philosophy contained so many revolutionary critical elements as Hegel's *Aesthetik*.

• According to Hegel, both bourgeois society and the Christian state are unfavourable to the development of creative art. Two inferences may be drawn from this: either art must perish in order to save the 'Absolute State', or the latter must be abolished in order to permit a new condition of the world, and a new renaissance of art. Hegel himself inclined to the first alternative. But with a slight change of emphasis the doctrine of the anti-aesthetic spirit of reality could readily assume a revolutionary character; and indeed Hegel's *Aesthetik* was thus interpreted by his radical followers whom Marx joined in 1837. On the other hand, Hegel's teachings concerning the decadence of art was considered by the liberal-bourgeois opposition to be insufficiently revolutionary and at the same time too dangerous. Hegel was simultaneously accused of lip-service to the Prussian government, Jacobinism, Bonapartism and even Saint-Simonism.

Marx's renunciation of romanticism and his acceptance of the basic tenets of Hegelian aesthetics thus signified a transition to a higher stage of political consciousness.

2

Marx's first work as a follower of Hegel was a dissertation on late Greek philosophy, particularly Epicureanism.[16]

In the various intellectual currents of antiquity in its period of decline, the Left Hegelians saw a close analogy to their own time. 'It seems strange', wrote Mehring, 'that this ideological vanguard of the bourgeoisie, which sought to develop the national existence of the German people, should have strengthened its self-consciousness by means of an ancient parallel originating in the disintegration of national existence.' The fact is, however—and this Mehring failed to understand—that there are 'two bourgeoisies', as Lenin said, and two ways of becoming aware of 'national existence'. Where the radical Hegelians rose to political insight, they defended the interests of democracy as opposed to those of liberalism. But these philosophical *montagnards* (to use Ruge's phrase) were convinced—as bourgeois democrats usually are—that every vestige of bourgeois relations, and social injustice in general, would vanish with the downfall of privileged capitalism, closely connected with the 'old regime'. Thus, the individual representatives of 'this ideological vanguard of the bourgeoisie' became more pronouncedly anti-bourgeois the more they were permeated

[16] *Differenz der demokritischen und epikureischen Naturphilosophie* (The Difference between the Democritean and Epicurean Philosophy of Nature), MEGA, I, I/1, pp1-144
The dissertation itself is available in English in Norman D Livergood, *Activity in Marx's Philosophy*, Martinus Nijhof, The Hague 1967, pp55-109

with the interest of a certain bourgeois stratum, to wit the petty bourgeoisie. Hence their criticism of bourgeois 'egoism' could not rise to a 'universal' point of view; hence their attacks on 'private interests' and atomistic disunity. To counteract these forces, which threatened to weaken all social ties, they proposed a 'plastic' unifying element of political relations.

We should not forget, however, that Marx occupied a unique position among the Hegelian idealists. Suffice it to recall his attitude toward ancient materialism.

The philosophy of Epicurus was not in favour among German idealists. Hegel repeatedly attacked him directly and indirectly. He considered his atomic principle an extreme expression of individualist society, in which each individual is isolated from the rest, and knows only the conflict of private interests, 'the war of all against all'. It was atomism, Hegel believed, as realized in economics and politics, which had brought about the decomposition of the 'kingdom of sublime morality', as he described Greek society. But when social life disintegrates, under the influence of the 'empirical freedom' of the individual, there remains only inner freedom, ideal life, self-analysis. This true freedom, as opposed to egoistic anarchy, was represented, according to Hegel, in Stoicism, and later in Christianity.

Marx's dissertation on Epicurus' physics was also a criticism of atomism and 'atomistic society'. But his view of Epicurus, Stoicism and Christianity was altogether different from Hegel's. And this difference, revealing as it does the abyss between the last representative of classical bourgeois philosophy and the founder-to-be of scientific socialism, is of great importance in understanding Marx's aesthetic views.

The foundation of Greek life—wrote Marx in his notes—was unity with nature. The history of antiquity was largely the history of the destruction of this unity. 'The degradation and profanation of nature meant in essence a disintegration of genuine life.' In this disintegration art itself became an instrument. Greek philosophy's poetical view of nature gave way to a mechanistic view of nature; the beautiful, integrated world of Homer came to be a mere façade hiding dry, quantitative relationships. Everything simple becomes complex, and everything complex inclines to disorganization. The cosmos falls into a multitude of finite bodies struggling for independence. These primary bodies are atoms. 'The formation of combinations of atoms, their repulsion and attraction, is noisy. Clamorous struggle and hostile tension fill the workshops and smithies of the world. The world is rent with tumult to its innermost depths. Even a sunbeam invading a shady spot is a symbol of this eternal conflict.'[17] This 'sonorous struggle of the atoms', reflecting so vividly the decay of the ancient world, attains its highest development in Rome. Roman poetry is quite unlike Greek poetry. 'Lucretius was a truly Roman epic poet, for he extolled the essence of the Roman spirit; instead of the serene, powerful, fulsome images of Homer, we find here solidly armed, invulnerable heroes, war *omnium contra omnes*, stern egotism, god-less nature, and un-worldly gods.'[18]

In all this Marx has not yet progressed beyond Hegel's *History of Philosophy*. Not until he analyzes the meaning of the atomic principle do new elements appear. Granted that this world of countless bodies contains inner contradictions. The atom is 'the full' as opposed to 'the empty': it is matter. It is subject to 'dependent motion', to falling down. But at the same time as an absolute unit the atom is free and independent. In emphasizing this distinction, Marx had in mind the contrast between material necessity and formal civic liberty, or, in the language of the Young Hegelians, between 'bourgeois society' and the 'political state'. Figuratively speaking, the atom as an aspect of materiality is nothing but a bourgeois; as an absolute form of existence it is a citizen of the French Revolution. Epicurus had emphasized the principle of atomicity,

[17] *ibid*, p124
[18] *ibid*, p126

that is, independence and hence individual freedom; but the contradictions of this principle were obvious even in his 'atomistic science'.

Within a complex body the atom cannot remain an isolated particle. As a unit it becomes a focus for all the richness of the outside world; it acquires additional qualities. But then it ceases to be merely an atom; its atomic form, as such, ceases to exist. In this analysis we find already the first formulation, however vague, of the position later to be taken in *The Holy Family*. To quote: 'Strictly and prosaically speaking, a member of society is not an atom at all.' Thus, the political poetry of a 'civic society' which presupposes the existence of completely equal and independent atom-citizens was questioned as early as in the Dissertation. The contradiction in the 'atomic principle' is that the independence and unity of the 'indivisible' disappear as soon as the atom partakes of real life.

Quite in the spirit of classical German philosophy, Marx took the opportunity in his Dissertation to discuss metaphorically some basic contemporary socio-political problems. In the doctrine of atomism he saw reflected the principle of the isolated private individual and the independent political citizen, a principle triumphantly brought forth by the French Revolution. The contrast between bourgeois-democratic ideals and the realities of life which grew apparent immediately after and even during the revolution, Marx, as a follower of Hegel, deduced from the concepts of the 'atom' and 'self-existence'.

A genuine atom exists only in the abstract, *in vacuo*, in the empty principles of the Constitution of 1793. 'Abstract individuality', wrote Marx, 'is freedom from existence, not freedom in existence. It cannot shine in the light of existence. In this medium it loses its character and becomes material.'[19]

A world of uniform and independent atom-citizens fears life because any real motion, any manifestation of living forces and interests, menaces its abstract equilibrium.

[19] *ibid*, p40. In Livergood, *op cit*, p95

This idea was expressed by Greek idealists as early as the fifth century B.C. 'Disregarding living forces, the idealist thinkers of that period [the Pythagoreans and the Eleatics] glorified the life of the state as the expression of reason.' Not satisfied with the current of actual life, these wise men turned against 'the reality of substance as manifested in the life of the people', and insisted on the 'right to ideal life'.

In order to clarify the dichotomy between the philosophico-political ideal and actuality, Marx employed an example from Epicurean theology. Epicurus expressed the idea of individual freedom in his doctrine of atomic 'declination', a notion which permeates his entire philosophy. It implies a refusal to participate in real life. 'Hence the goal of action is abstraction, ataraxy, avoidance of pain and disturbance. Hence the good is escape from evil; pleasure is the avoidance of suffering.'[20] The principle of declination attains its highest expression in Epicurean theology: 'Much fun has been made of Epicurus' gods, who, though they resemble men, inhabit the intermundane spaces of the real world, who have a *quasi* body instead of a body and *quasi* blood instead of blood, and who, being frozen in blissful calm, hearken to no prayer, worry about neither us nor the world, and are worshipped for their beauty, majesty and perfect nature rather than for any selfish motives. And yet these gods were no fiction of Epicurus' invention. They existed. They were the sculptured gods of Greek art. Cicero, the Roman, was justified in mocking them; but Plutarch, the Greek, completely forgot all Greek conceptions when he declared that this theory of the gods suppresses fear and superstition because it attributes to the gods neither joy nor benevolence, but places them in the same relationship to us as the Hyrcanean fish, from which we expect neither help nor harm. Theoretical calm was one of the outstanding characteristics of the Greek gods, as Aristotle pointed out, saying: "The perfectly conditioned has no need of action, since it is itself the end." '[21]

[20] *ibid*, p29. In Livergood, *op cit*, p82
[21] *ibid*, p30. In Livergood, *op cit*, p82

3

This interpretation of Greek sculpture was already a step in the direction of a denial of Hegelian idealism. In subsequent polemics with Stirner who, in the customary manner of German speculative philosophy, represented antiquity as an epoch of the domination of the 'flesh' over the 'spirit', Marx remarked: 'The ancients, as portrayed by idealist political historians, are "citizens", while the moderns are mere "bourgeois", realistic "amis du commerce".' This aspect of ancient reality Marx found expressed, as we have already noted, in the portrayal of the Greek gods—calm, indifferent, abhorrent of practicality and change—change inseparable from world trade, money, modern social relations. But precisely here lay the secret of the inevitable doom of Greek art, precisely here lay its historical limitations. The underground forces feared by the ancient city-state demolished the stone walls of the Acropolis, and with it collapsed the plastic qualities of Greek art; thenceforth the gods dwelt in the 'intermundane spaces' of Epicurean religion.

Following the classical period, characterized by 'the dialectics of measure', came the reign of contradictions, deterioration. 'We should not forget that such catastrophes are succeeded by the age of iron—a fortunate age if characterized by a titanic struggle, but a pitiful one if devoted to reproducing in wax, gypsum or bronze the pieces of marble created in the manner of Pallas Athene sprung from the head of Zeus.' Eras such as the Roman are 'unfortunate and iron'; then the 'spirit cannot help but retreat into private life'.

This interpretation was undoubtedly influenced by Hegel's *Aesthetik* and *History of Philosophy*. For example, Marx's contention that there was a connection between the ideal of the political unity of atom-'citizens' and Greek sculpture probably derived from Hegel's doctrine of the deterioration of the 'classical ideal'. Political liberty was supposedly a condition of the efflorescence of Greek art. Consequently with the downfall of Greek democracy Greek sculpture was bound to deteriorate. The Olympic gods were defeated by the same contradiction—the antinomy between *the one and the many*. The gods of Greek art constituted a plastic unity. Yet each of them had its distinctive form, individuality, a corporeal existence. Hence, conflict of individual interests, discord, multiplicity. The gods turned away from the tumult of living passions and retired into the repose of sculpture. Hence the grief of their majestic countenances. 'The gods grieve', said Hegel, 'because of their own corporeality. In their images we perceive their destiny: the contrast between universality and particularity, the spiritual and the sensuous, leads classic art to its decay.'

While Marx shared Hegel's theory that the deterioration of ancient democracy and the decline of Greek sculpture were alike due to the conflict of material interests, within the general outlines of this view there was an essential difference between them. In order to understand this point in Marx's Dissertation, it must be recalled that the Jacobins' attempt to restore ancient democracy had exerted a tremendous influence upon German philosophy of the time, but this attempt had foundered on the conflict of interests, on the economic relations of bourgeois society. As an absolute idealist, Hegel interpreted this historical conflict as a contradiction between the ideal nature of spirit and the material elements of actual life. Herein lay the reason, he thought, for the decline of classical art, too sensuous for the spirit of a new age turning inward. This decay, according to Hegel, represented a fatal process in which external form gives way before the higher development of spiritual content. The combination of freedom and life, as it existed among the citizens of the republics of antiquity, was due to an insufficient development of the 'cosmic spirit'. And when, upon its further growth, material reality was purged of liberty—in the philosophical schools of later antiquity as well as in Christianity—liberty was transformed into inner liberty, freedom from external reality. This historical contradiction, in Hegel's opinion, expresses the eternal triumph of the spirit over its material raiment. It was not, therefore, the idealism of Greek sculpture which caused its decadence, but on the contrary its unity with nature, its living warmth. Thus the final word of Hegel's aesthetics was, as Marx said, not 'freedom in existence' but 'freedom from existence'.

In his Dissertation Marx on the whole adhered to Hegel's absolute idealism; however, he introduced a substantial correction into the Hegelian interpretation of the fall of the ancient world, and he drew an entirely different conclusion from the experience of the French Revolution. The decline of Greek democracy was brought about not by the realism of antiquity (where, according to Marx's *German Ideology* 'communal life was a "truth", whereas in modern times it has become an idealistic lie'). Quite the contrary, the seed of its destruction lay in the idealism of abstract civic freedom, which is incapable of mastering material development. *The historical limitation of ancient sculpture was not its adherence to life, its corporeality, but on the contrary, its escape from life, its retreat into empty space.* 'Abstract individuality', i.e. the atom of 'civic society', 'cannot shine in the light of existence'. The only conclusion which can be drawn from this interpretation is that freedom and material life must be united around a higher principle than the 'abstract individuality' of the atom-citizen. Or, to translate philosophy into the language of politics, democratic demands must be given a realistic plebeian colouring, a broad mass base. Such is the latent tendency of Marx's work on the natural philosophy of Epicurus. Democracy without political idealism, or political idealism with democracy—herein lies the difference between Marx and Hegel.

Hence the two thinkers' distinctive evaluations of Epicurus. For Hegel, Epicurus' atomism, particularly his doctrine of atomic declination (i.e. that atoms fall not vertically but in deviation from the straight line), represented the principle of the empirical 'ego', the arbitrariness of individual action destroying the unity of ancient citizenship. Marx, on the other hand, interpreted the doctrine of atomic declination altogether differently. He restored Epicurus as an enlightened thinker who discovered in egoism the foundation of human society. In deviating in its descent, the atom manifests self-love, personal interests, but it is only through this deviation that it can meet other atoms in space and form various combinations with them. Mutual repulsion creates the sociality of atoms. 'In the realm of politics this constitutes the social contract, in communal life—friendship.'[22] Thus atomism and egoism are overcome through personal development. A similar deduction of general will [*volonté générale*] from correctly understood egoism was drawn by the French materialists of the eighteenth century, as well as by Feuerbach and Chernishevsky. Lenin, too, saw in this concept 'the starting point of historical materialism'.

Epicurus was the first theoretician of the 'social contract'. He was, therefore, a Rousseauist before Rousseau, a precursor of the French Revolution. The principle of egoism admits of two alternatives. It may be the egoism of 'private interest', seeking exclusive domination and oligarchy, such as Robespierre and his government fought against. Or on the other hand, it may be the egoism of revolutionary toilers opposing unsocial acts on the part of citizens: the mass egoism of peasants wishing to divide the landowners' estates or that of industrial workers demanding better conditions of work and freedom from em-

[22] *ibid*, p32. In Livergood, *op cit*, p85

B

ployers' whims. Such is the revolutionary dialectic of the 'principle of atomism', its self-negation and transition to a higher level. All this is to be found in Marx's Dissertation, in a latent form, of course, and wrapped in a heavy blanket of Hegelian idealism.

That which had its origin in the 'disintegration of national existence' (to use Mehring's expression) in modern times acquired an almost opposite signficance. That is why Marx, in seeking 'to develop the national existence of the German people', in seeking, that is, to solve the basic problem of the bourgeois-democratic revolution in Germany, turned to the dying world of antiquity.

'New philosophy stands upon the ground where ancient philosophy perished,' wrote Marx. That which was a product of the disintegration of the Greek world view in modern times became 'a rational view of nature'. 'That which formerly was a profanation of nature now becomes a liberation from the fetters imposed by faith.' Epicurean philosophy, in the olden days signifying a retreat into private life, now became the banner of a 'titanic struggle' against celestial and terrestrial deities 'who refuse to acknowledge human self-consciousness as divine'. Correspondingly, Hegel's doctrine of the 'irrevocable passing away of the kingdom of sublime morality' in Marx's hands received a novel emphasis. 'Now surely it is a very trivial truth that birth, maturation and death constitute the iron circle within which everything human is perforce confined and through which it must pass. . . . Death itself is preformed in living; it must therefore be understood as a specific form of life.'[23] In a letter to his father written in November 1837, Marx described his time as a period of transition. 'Every metamorphosis', he wrote, 'is to some extent a swan song, to some extent the overture to a great new poem.'[24] As we shall see in the pages following, Karl

[23] *ibid*, p13-14. In Livergood, *op cit*, p62
[24] Marx, letter to his father, 10 November 1837, *op cit* (footnote 6), p41

Marx endeavoured to transform the 'swan song' of the old world—Hegelian philosophy—into 'the overture to a great new poem'.

4

Marx's Dissertation was fundamentally an analysis of two possible aspects of Epicurean philosophy: (1) passive retreat into private life, and (2) the subsequent bourgeois 'enlightenment' with its 'titanic struggle' against religious and political oppression. To the publicists of the Left-Hegelian wing, the Epicurean world view was symbolic of the constant vacillation of certain elements of the bourgeoisie between apathetic apoliticism and nationalistic-democratic trends. But just then, in the early forties, when Marx was writing the last pages of his Dissertation, the liberal, romantically-minded crown prince Frederick William IV ascended the Prussian throne, and the German middle class was filled with illusions of beneficent reform from above.

In these circumstances Marx decided to make closer contact with Bruno Bauer and his group, who at that time were attacking the half-way policies of German liberals such as Schleiermacher, Weisse and Strauss, as well as conservative Hegelians ready to exchange their master's dialectics for pietistic liberalism.

The Left Hegelians found it necessary to distinguish between the progressive aspects of Hegel's philosophy and its religious philistine side. Therefore they issued anonymously two parodic pamphlets 'exposing' Hegel as a Jacobin and an atheist: *Die Posaune des jüngsten Gerichtes über Hegel, den Atheisten und Antichristen. Ein Ultimatum* [The Trumpet of the Last Judgment against Hegel, the

Atheists and the Anti-Christs][25] and *Hegels Lehre von der Religion und Kunst vom dem Standpunkt des Glaubens ausbeurteilt* [Hegel's Teachings on Religion and Art from the Standpoint of Faith].[26] While these pamphlets were written by Bauer, Marx participated in their composition, having been assigned to write a full section dealing with art[27] in a second pamphlet. Marx devoted the entire winter of 1841-42 to this work. In the spring, however, he abandoned the undertaking with the intention of re-writing his treatise *Uber Religion und Kunst mit besondrer Beziehung auf christliche Kunst* [On Religion and Art with special reference to Christian Art] as two independent articles, *Uber religiose Kunst* [On Religious Art] and *Uber die Romantiker* [On the Romantics]. These articles are not extant, but the basic principles of the treatise can be reconstructed from the anonymous pamphlets of 1841-42 and from Marx's notations on books read while working on the treatise.

The two pamphlets constitute primarily an apology for the French Revolution and particularly its extreme, terrorist party. This point is especially remarkable since all the historical sources available to Marx and Bauer were permeated with hatred toward the Jacobins—the first exoneration of Robespierre, undertaken by Buchez in his *Histoire Parlementaire de la Révolution Française*, was only then appearing in France.

In these satirical pamphlets Hegel is depicted as a faithful follower of the Terrorists. 'Hegel envies the French nation for its bloody revolutionary bath!' exclaims a Hegelian disguised as a pious man. 'He considers the French people the Messiah of all nations, and revolution the only salvation of humanity.' He despises the Germans,

---

[25] Published by O Wigand, Leipzig 1841
[26] Published by O Wigand, Leipzig 1842
[27] This section was entitled *'Hegels Hass gegen die religiose und christliche Kunst und seine Auflösung aller positiven Staatsgesetze'* (Hegel's hatred of religious and Christian art and his dissolution of all positive state laws)

the pamphlet continues, for their attachment to the night-cap, their pedantry, their slavish passivity. The only real followers of Hegel are that 'gang of Left Hegelians'. But they are not Germans at all, they are Frenchmen. 'No wonder these persons admire the French Revolution; no wonder they study its history—they wish to imitate it. And who knows, perhaps among them there is already a Danton, a Marat, a Robespierre?'!

Because of his antipathy for religion and government, Hegel extols antiquity. 'Hegel is a great friend of Greek religion and of the Greeks. He exalts above all the Hellenic faith, which essentially is no religion at all. But he calls it *the religion of beauty, art, freedom, humanity* . . . Hegel finds humaneness, liberty, morality and individuality in only one religion, a religion which is not really a religion —the religion of art, in which man worships himself. Real religion, in which everything is God and God's worship, seems to him too sombre. The real God he considers a sombre, morose and jealous tyrant, God's servant a *selfish slave* who serves others in order to maintain his meagre existence among the miseries of this world.'

Thus the French Revolution and Greek art were contrasted, by the Left-Hegelian pamphleteers, with the prosaic morality, so inimical to art, of the Old Testament. It must be understood, however, that their attack on the dry and sombre egoism of the Pentateuch was not merely a belated polemic against Mosaic laws. In contrasting the Oriental world outlook with classical art, the Left Hegelians really referred to the old Testament of feudal-bourgeois Germany, with its system of privilege and greed. The new barbarism of capitalist Germany is identified with the barbarism of old. The God of monotheistic religion is the monstrous image of an egoistic individual engaged in the satisfaction of his own material wants. And in the realm of sensuousness and greed there is no room for form, beauty and art.

Fetishistic worship of the external world differentiates the Greek realm of art from the Oriental realm of religion.

Instead of a theoretical attitude toward nature we find bare practicality, instead of aesthetic craftsmanship, rapacity and crudity, instead of personal freedom and citizenship, privilege and despotism.

'No real individuality, no real personality is possible in this despotic kingdom; human freedom and self-consciousness are ostracized, and with them is lost the only real source of art as well as of history' (Hegel's *Aesthetik*).

Under these conditions, man can do nothing but submit. Aesthetic contemplation is simply unthinkable. 'When the gods are endowed with the sole right of decision, human independence—the prerequisite of artistic ideals—suffers. According to Christian doctrine, the Holy Spirit guides man toward God. But then the spirit of man is mere passive soil acted upon by the divine will; the human will is destroyed as a free agency. If, on the contrary, man is opposed to the Deity, then their relation is prosaic: God commands, and man has no other choice but to obey' [Hegel's *Aesthetik*]. Thus the home of the ancient citizen was the 'art studio', whereas the home of the pious man is 'an asylum for beggars and feebleminded'.

Let us now turn to Marx's notebooks, which contain synopses of books read in the early part of 1842.[28] These notes reveal the main features of Marx's revolutionary-democratic beliefs. Much of what is contained here does not completely disappear in his later development, although it leads to deeper insights.

The origin of art lies in free, organic social life. 'If we consider the gods and heroes of Greek art *without religious or aesthetic prejudices*, we find in them nothing that could not exist in the pulsations of nature. Indeed, these images are artistic only as they portray *beautiful human mores* in a splendid integrated form.'[29]

On the other hand, oppression and fear, slavery and

[28] Charles Debrosses, *Über den Dienst der Fetischgötter*; Johann Jakob Grund, *Die Malerei der Griechen*; C F von Rumohr, *Italienische Forschungen*—M L
[29] Marginal note in Rumohr, p124—M L

tyranny, call for that which is inimical to art. 'Everything ugly and monstrous despises art. But nevertheless the portrayal of the gods among ancient nations was never altered. Wherever they were given a perfectly natural portrayal, we find that such treatment received no development. This is because in so far as fear entered into the various conceptions of the gods, and in so far as such gods sanctified the origin of the various social groups, the leaders of such groups found in this fear a means of controlling the populace; in other words, they made this fear of god the citadel of their domination, spreading it among the people and preserving unchanged the ugly, fear-inspiring images of the gods. Since fear paralyzes the mind, people educated and held in fear can never develop and elevate their minds; quite the contrary, the innate ability to imitate and hence acquire artistic feelings, becomes almost completely repressed.'[30] A supernatural agency dominating man by inspiring fear cannot be endowed with natural, human attributes. Hence distorted features, arbitrary symbols of mythical concepts such as wings, together with essentially natural forms of angels and saints.[31] The more primitive, distorted and ugly a piece of art, the cruder its workmanship, the greater, it seems, is its religious significance. Marx made a list of passages from Debrosses' famous book on fetishism, indicating lack of artistic workmanship as a condition of religious worship. For instance, the figure of Hercules in one of the temples of Beotia, 'far from being a work of art, was merely a crude stone image of ancient origin'. And even after the art of portraying the human body in sculpture had made considerable progress, religious worship remained faithful to the shapeless old stones. For, according to Pausanias, 'the ugliest, like the oldest, deserves the greatest respect'.[32]

This peculiarity of religious feeling was made a principle of Christian art. Marx made a note of the following

[30] Marginal note in Grund, Vol I, p4—ML
[31] Rumohr, p125—ML
[32] Debrosses, p117—ML

passage on Gothic sculpture by Grund: 'Sculpture lived mainly from the alms of architecture. Statues of saints filled the interior and exterior walls of buildings; in their multiplicity they expressed the excess of worship: small in appearance lean and angular in shape, awkward and unnatural in pose, they were below any real artistry, just as man, their creator, was below himself.'[33]

Thus we find in Marx's notebooks the same contrasts observed in the satirical pamphlets of 1841-42. On the one hand, the realism of ancient art based upon the democracy of the Greek republics; on the other hand, the Oriental religious outlook based upon oppression and submission. Christian art of the post-classical period reproduced on a new level the aesthetics of Asiatic barbarism. There was a contact between Christian and Oriental culture. Arbitrary elongation and broadening of forms, love for the colossal and grandiose, characterized the art of both cultures. In classical art, form and artistry are essential; but the religious view strives after simple quantity, formless matter. Marx's notebooks contain many references to this point. Christian architecture sought exaggeration and loftiness; yet it was lost in barbaric pomp and countless details. 'The whole is overburdened with excess and splendour.'[34]

Religious art was marked by mathematical logic and dryness, rather than organic form created by artistic imagination. For instance, the earliest Greek statues, reflecting the influence of Egyptian patterns, were mere 'models of the mathematical construction of the body', containing no elements of beauty, because in them 'nature was subordinated to reason rather than to the imagination'.[35] In Christian art that which was truly religious was represented by rational symbols, celestial mechanics and abstract allegories. The early Christians seemed to prefer simple, non-artistic symbolism to depiction of reality. In so far as painting (in the fifteenth century) liberated itself from re-

[33] Grund, Vol I, p15—ML
[34] ibid—ML
[35] ibid, p24—ML

ligious subjects, it preferred various domestic scenes, though still concerned with saints.

An idea which was of tremendous significance in Marx's entire subsequent development can be traced back to his notebooks of 1842. This is the idea of 'fetishism'. When, in later years, speaking of commodity fetishism, Marx turned for an analogy to the 'nebulous world of religion', he had in mind that very trait of the religious outlook which in the treatise of 1842 figured as the fundamental cause of the antagonism between art and religion. *The fetishistic character of religion is demonstrated by the fact that it worships the material aspect of things, endowing them with the qualities of man himself.* It is often thought that these objects of worship are mere symbols, into which meaning is read by the worshippers themselves. This is not so, however. The objects of fetishistic cult worship are not *symbols* but *realities*, not *forms* but *things*. In their materiality, as such, man perceives a source of well-being; their natural image is an expression of his own powers.

Wherever art endows the gods with human form, fetishists immediately identify the deified power with its image. 'A sensuous man wanted to see in the image, god in person, to enjoy realistic possession. Some ancient nations hoped to find their safety and well-being in the image of a god-protector.' Sensuous men, i.e. fetishists, believe that 'the deity lives in its image, that the image is god'.[36] Hence their behaviour with regard to the fetish, so expressive of greed and lust, of hypocrisy and crude practicality.

All artistic workmanship, all theoretical, disinterested concern with natural objects, is foreign to fetishism. In Greek poetry and art man's creative abilities gave form to things, but religious egoism knows only a predatory attitude toward nature.

Such, in the main, is the content of Marx's notebooks. The fundamental thesis of the treatise on Christian art was thus the antithesis between the ancient principle of form and the fetishistic worship of materiality. The crude

[36] *ibid*, pp183-184—ML

naturalism and practicality of the fetishistic world were contrasted with the creative activity of man. Marx at that time was still far from understanding that the newest fetishism was itself a product of a definite mode of production. And so we do not find in the excerpts of 1842 anything even remotely resembling Marx's later views on the historical disproportion between the development of the productive forces of society and its artistic growth. Quite the contrary, art and technical skill here appear united in their opposition to archaic and modern barbarism.

As we have already seen, the defence of Greek art was at the same time an attempt to restore the ideals of the French Revolution. Like the Jacobins in France, the Left Hegelians criticized 'bourgeois egoism' and the 'aristocracy of capital'—vaguely distinguished from the aristocracy by the grace of God. If the connection between aesthetic and social criticism remains somewhat hazy in the excerpts belonging to the Bonn period, it becomes clear in Marx's journalistic writings of 1842.

5

Disappointed in the new government, the Prussian bourgeoisie turned left, seeking to assume leadership of the new democratic movement in Germany. Agitation in favour of the *Zollverein* [Customs Union] was infused with purely political propaganda; the bourgeoisie attempted to speak in the language of the citizenry.

In these new conditions, the Left Hegelians' criticism of the liberals and the bourgeoisie revealed its short-comings. Most of the radical members of the Hegelian school, beneath a superficial layer of criticism directed against bourgeois progress, were really quite attached to the patriarchal traditions of German life and ideology. For this reason Marx, seeking a broader foundation for revolutionary-democratic ideas, established temporary contact with the progressive bourgeois party. In the pages of the *Rheinische Zeitung* (which Marx at first contributed to, and later edited, until it was suppressed by the government early in 1843), he sought to transform the opposition of the German bourgeoisie into a real democratic, nation-wide movement. This coalition with the progressive bourgeoisie eventually cost him the friendship of Bruno Bauer and the 'Freemen', who preferred to stay aloof from a popular movement and to pose as a sort of Jacobin club and atheist salon.

In his criticism of bourgeois liberalism, Marx did not tread the path of political romanticism, as Bauer did.[37] On

[37] Cf Marx's letter to Engels, 18 January 1856, *Selected Correspondence,* edited by Dona Torr, London 1934, pp77-78

the contrary, he criticized liberalism precisely for its romanticism, which served to disguise the crudest and most barbaric forms of oppression and exploitation. After the final bankruptcy of the old absolute monarchy, the policy of Frederick William IV was to direct the development of German capitalism along the so-called 'Prussian way'. Romanticism became the official ideology of this new policy. In the early forties it triumphed everywhere, from the royal offices to the University of Berlin, where the dominating influence was the aged Schelling.

By this time romanticism, as a politico-aesthetic doctrine, had undergone a typical evolution. Originally a middle-class opposition to the 'enlightened absolutism' of the eighteenth century, in the first half of the nineteenth century it became a theoretical prop of the Holy Alliance. Nor did the romantic reaction stop with open support of feudal landownership. It also appealed to the bourgeoisie, attempting to prove that medieval urban 'liberties' were much closer to the real spirit of bourgeois ownership than the 'liberty' and 'equality' of the French Revolution. On the other hand it also tried to utilize the lower strata of the population in its struggle against the progressive bourgeoisie, who had adopted the idea of 'enlightenment'. In this complicated system of liberal gestures combined with police kicks, romantic doctrines occupied a rather prominent place.

Romanticism in politics, science and art, was the archenemy of the *Rheinische Zeitung*. The political role of romanticism was discussed in an anonymous article as follows: 'Fantastic depiction of the emotions can pervert any people who are insufficiently enlightened. It has the same effect as mysticism and pietism. . . . Everything ordinary and human it replaces with the excessive, everything harmonious and organized, with the arbitrary.'[38] Referring to an article by Marx directed against the historical school of law, also published in the *Rheinische Zeitung*, the

---

[38] *Rheinische Zeitung*, No 254, 1842—ML

author asserts that the customary interpretation of romanticism as a reaction against the frivolous tendencies of the eighteenth century, is erroneous. Nineteenth-century romanticism was, on the contrary, a continuation of the frivolous mood of the privileged classes.

The anonymous writer was quite justified in referring to Marx. The discrepancy between the poetical form and the prosaic content, the liberal exterior and the reactionary essence of romanticism, did indeed interest Marx very deeply in 1842. As we have already seen, he intended to devote a special section of his treatise on Christian art to romanticism. With the help of articles written in 1842 it is not difficult to reconstruct the basic tenets of his criticism of romanticism.

Throughout these articles there runs the central thought that the 'perverted world' of plutocracy and aristocracy inevitably generates a host of illusions, fantasies and fictions. Unlike Left Hegelians such as Bauer, Marx even then sought the objective basis for these inventions in social relations. The upholders of the 'Christian-knightly, modern-feudal—in short, romantic—principle', wrote Marx, cannot comprehend 'that which is in itself incomprehensible', namely how freedom can be 'the *individual privilege* of certain persons and certain classes': how the right of social man to be free can be embodied, therefore, in 'certain human individuals', as, for example, sovereignty is embodied in the physical nature of a monarch. Failing to comprehend this, 'they are forced to seek refuge in the *miraculous* and the *mystical.* And since, furthermore, the *real* situation of these gentlemen in the modern state does not in the least correspond to what they imagine it to be, because of the fact that they live in a world located *outside reality*, and because their imagination is therefore substituted for their head and heart, they must perforce cling, not being satisfied with practice, to a theory, but to a *theory of the Beyond*—to religion, which in their hand always acquires a polemical bitterness, impregnated with political tendencies, and becomes, more or less consciously, simply a sacred veil to hide utterly profane, but at the same time fantastic desires.'[39]

Romanticism wraps in glory even that which is in reality dry, prosaic fact. The noble pretensions of romanticism are in vivid contrast to its underlying callousness. Hence the hypocrisy of romanticism, 'which is always, at the same time, *tendentious poetry*'.[40] Marx's contempt for romanticism remained undiminished to the end. His attitude towards Chateaubriand is typical. In 1854 he wrote to Engels: 'In my leisure moments I am now studying Spanish. I began with Calderón; from his *Mágico Prodigioso*—the Catholic *Faust*—Goethe took not only certain passages, but even the sequence of whole scenes for his Faust. Then I read—*horrible dictu!*—in Spanish, something which I could never have read in French, Chateaubriand's *Atala and René*, and some extracts from Bernardin de Saint-Pierre.'[41] In another letter to Engels we find a brief analysis of this branch of romanticism: 'In studying the Spanish cesspool, I fell upon the manipulations of the worthy Chateaubriand, that manufacturer of belles lettres who unites, in a most obnoxious manner, the polite scepticism and Voltairianism of the eighteenth century with the polite sentimentalism and romanticism of the nineteenth. This union could not fail to be epoch-making in France *from the point of view of style*, although even in the style the falseness is often glaringly obvious, despite the artistic artifices.'[42]

Marx's denunciation of the hypocrisy of Chateaubriand's creed, which combined *sober scepticism* with *romantic sentimentality*, is consistent with what he had written as far back as 1842; and his interpretation of 'ro-

---

[39] *Debatten über Pressfreiheit* (Debates on the Freedom of the Press), MEGA, I, I/1, pp198-199
[40] 'Comments on the Latest Prussian Censorship Instruction', in Easton and Guddat (eds), *op cit* (footnote 6), p88
[41] Marx, letter to Engels, 3 May 1854, MEGA, III, 2, p28
[42] Marx, letter to Engels, 26 October 1854, MEGA, III, 2, p58

mantic culture' remained unchanged, as can be seen from
the following fragment belonging to the seventies: 'I have
just read Sainte-Beuve's book on Chateaubriand, a writer
who has always repelled me. If this man has become so
celebrated in France, it is because he is from every point
of view the most classical embodiment of French *vanité*
—and because he clothes this *vanité* not in the light and
frivolous costume of the eighteenth century, but in the
romantic costume, and makes it strut in a newly-created
style; here one finds false profundity, Byzantine exaggeration, sentimental coquetry, multicoloured iridescence, word
painting, the theatrical, the *sublime*, in short a medley
of lies such as never before existed either in form or in
content.'[43]

[43] Marx, letter to Engels, 30 November 1873, MEGA, III, 3,
p409

6

In his discussion of the censorship edict of 1841[44] Marx demonstrated the utterly specious character of 'romantic culture', its ostensible humaneness masking its actual oppression. The practical, frankly egoistic regime of Frederick William iii had required from newspaper editors a monetary guarantee of good behaviour. His liberal-romantic successor substituted for the pecuniary and prosaic guarantee an idealistic pledge having a purely imaginary significance. Instead of money, the new royal regulation required of editors 'literary ability' and 'social status'. 'To require literary ability—what a broad and liberal measure!' exclaimed Marx. 'To require status, what a narrow and illiberal measure! But to require both literary ability and social status—that's but the semblance of liberalism!'[45] Beneath the gloss of romanticism we often find private interest and self-interest. On the question of freedom of the press, the Prussian king's romantic instructions were that the matter be entrusted wholly to the censor. The writer and the editor were not the least bit protected, even by some legal arrangement, from the whim of the censor. The same hypocrisy was to be found in the debates concerning the law against the pilfering of wood.[46]

Nobility of purpose plus utter callousness character-

[44] 'Comments on the Latest Prussian Censorship Instruction', in Easton and Guddat (eds), *op cit* (footnote 6), pp67-92
[45] *ibid*, p88
[46] *Debatten über das Holzdiebstahlsgesetz* (Debates on the Wood-theft Laws), MEGA, I, I/1, pp266-304

izes 'self-interest' in all stages of its development. Consider, for instance, the bourgeoisie's righteous indignation against factory laws, their romantic faith in the personal virtue of the bosses—especially when the interests of the workers are at stake,—together with their captious attention to the rules governing order within the factory. Not personal freedom, but rather its cruel subjugation, is the real basis of romantic 'self-interest'.

An excellent example of this, as Marx and Engels pointed out later in a review published in the *Revue der Neuen Rheinischen Zeitung*,[47] is Carlyle's romantic doctrine: 'Carlyle provides a striking illustration of how pompous balderdash turns into its opposite, how a noble, knowing and wise man in practice becomes a cad, an ignoramus and a fool.' Consider this argument of Carlyle's: 'In all European countries, especially in England, one class of captains and commanders of men, recognizable as the beginning of a new real and not imaginary "Aristocracy", has already in some measure developed itself: the Captains of Industry—happily the class who above all, or at least first of all, are wanted in this time. In the doing of material work, we have already men among us that can command bodies of men. And surely, on the other hand, there is no lack of men needing to be commanded: the sad class of brother-men whom we had to describe as "Hodge's emancipated horses", reduced to roving famine—this too has in all countries developed itself; and, in fatal geometrical progression, is ever more developing itself, with a rapidity which alarms every one. On this ground, if not on all manner of other grounds, it may be truly said, the "Organization of Labour" (*not* organizable by the mad methods tried hitherto) is the universal Problem of the world.'[48] Here Marx and Engels remark: 'After Carlyle on the first

[47] Review of Thomas Carlyle's *Latter-Day Pamphlets*. Cf Franz Mehring (ed), *Aus dem literarischen Nachlass von K Marx, F Engels, F Lassalle*, III, pp414-426

[48] Thomas Carlyle, *The Present Time, Latter-Day Pamphlets*, in *Carlyle's Works*, XVI, Boston 1901, p37

forty pages has thundered out all his righteous indignation against egoism, free competition, the abolition of feudal bonds between man and man, supply and demand, laissez faire, cotton spinning, interest payment, etc, etc, we suddenly find that the principal sponsors of all these shams, the industrial bourgeoisie, not only belong among the celebrated heroes and geniuses, but also comprise the next order of these heroes, that the trump card of all his attacks upon bourgeois relationships and ideas is the apotheosis of bourgeois personalities.'[49]

Marx and Engels subject Carlyle's hero worship to devastating criticism: 'The new era, in which genius reigns, is distinguished from the old chiefly by the fact that the whip imagines itself to be genius. Carlyle's genius is distinguished from any ordinary prison Cerberus or poorhouse superintendent by his righteous indignation and his moral conscience, which make him maltreat the poor solely in order to raise them to his own level. Here we see how, in his expiatory wrath, this genius who is so affirmative justifies and exaggerates fantastically the infamies of the bourgeois.'[50]

Years later Marx summed up his criticism of reactionary romanticism in the following manner: 'The same bourgeois mind which praises division of labour in the workshop, life-long annexation of the labourer to a partial operation, and his complete subjection to capital, as being an organization of labour that increases its productiveness —that same bourgeois mind denounces with equal vigour every conscious attempt to socially control and regulate the process of production, as an inroad upon such sacred things as the right of property, freedom and unrestricted play for the bent of the individual capitalist. It is very characteristic that the enthusiastic apologists of the factory system have nothing more damning to urge against a general organization of the labour of society,

---

[49] *Aus dem Literarischen Nachlass*, III, *op cit* (footnote 47)
[50] *ibid*

than that it would turn all society into one immense factory.'[51]

[51] Marx, *Capital*, I, Moscow 1959, p353

7

In 1842 Marx was not yet a revolutionist in the proletarian sense of that word. He regarded the democratic revolution, or, in the language of the forties, 'political emancipation', as the solution of all social problems. He did not yet discriminate between the medieval romanticism of privileged 'self-interest' and the fetishism of purely bourgeois relations. Morover, his starting point was still the *Aesthetik* of Hegel, who described as 'romantic' all the art of 'modern nations', be it a medieval miniature or a Dutch still life.

This confusion of feudalism's Reynard the Fox with the Darwinian 'beast' of bourgeois society was common to all Left Hegelians. However, whereas Bruno Bauer, for example, assailed bourgeois society as a product of the decadence of feudal-patriarchal society, Marx exposed feudal rottenness and decay as merely concealing bourgeois relations in Germany. Hence their confusion of 'political' emancipation with 'human' emancipation resulted in almost opposite interpretations. For Marx it was *Revolution in Permanenz,* continuation of the bourgeois-democratic revolution to its ultimate conclusion: for Bauer it was an attempt to circumvent the capitalist phase of development, a mere romantic criticism of the bourgeois-democratic revolution.

It would be a mistake to regard the young Marx as an ordinary bourgeois radical. While supporting the party of the Rhenish manufacturers and merchants against the romantic ghosts of the 'old regime', Marx nevertheless bitterly criticized the mercenary ethic of the bourgeoisie. Struggle against romanticism, a barrier in the path of bourgeois progress, and criticism of the cowardly egoism of the German bourgeoisie, represented for the young Marx but a single line of attack against all remnants of the middle ages.

Fulfilling its great historical mission and substituting 'exploitation veiled by religious and political illusions' with 'naked, shameless, direct, brutal exploitation', the bourgeoisie 'stripped of its halo every occupation hitherto honoured and looked up to with reverent awe', as Marx and Engels expressed it later in *The Communist Manifesto*.[52] Even the writer and poet could not escape this fate. The bourgeoisie converted the poet into its 'paid wagelabourer'. And although from a socio-historical point of view this represented a great forward stride, nevertheless it reduced literature to the level of a commodity. On the very next day after the writer's escape from the censor and his romantic caprices, there arose the danger that literature would be transformed into a mere trade, at the mercy of the moneybags. This danger Marx had already noted in his article on freedom of the press.

So far we have had to deal with the representatives of the modern-feudal form of the romantic principle. But now we are confronted with the representatives of 'self-interest' unvarnished by romanticism. These are the orators of the bourgeoisie belonging to the 'urban estate'. These people are always ready 'to explain the great by petty causes, and, assuming correctly that everything for which man struggles is concerned with his own interests, proceed to the incorrect conclusion that there are only "petty" interests, interests of stereotyped selfishness.'[53] Hence according to the viewpoint of the 'urban estate' the literary craft must come under the regulation of freedom of craft

[52] *Manifesto of the Communist Party*, in Marx-Engels, *Selected Works* (2 vol edition), I, Moscow 1958, p36

[53] *Debatten über Pressfreiheit* (Debates on the Freedom of the Press), MEGA, I, I/1, p218

in general. It was on this ground that the Diet speaker defended freedom of the press. 'The first thing that strikes us,' wrote Marx, 'is to see freedom of the press brought under the heading of freedom of craft. Yet we cannot reject the speaker's view forthwith. Rembrandt painted the Mother of God as a Dutch peasant woman: why should not our speaker paint freedom in the form with which he is familiar?'[54]

This removal of the fantastic halo surrounding literary activity was a progressive historic fact. However, there is another side to the matter. 'Correct as is the conclusion that the higher form of a law can be considered proved by the law of a lower form, the *application* is incorrect which makes the *lower sphere* the measure of the higher one and distorts its laws, sensible within their own limitations, into the comical by attributing to them the pretension of being laws not of their own spheres but of a superior sphere.'[55] The bourgeois, who is quite sober and prosaic when his own interests are at stake, tries to use in literature the same criterion which he applies to sugar, leather and bristle. He considers freedom of the press as a 'thing', and this is contrary to its character.

'In order to defend a particular freedom, to say nothing of comprehending it, I must grasp its essential characteristics rather than its external relations. Is a press true to its character, does it act in accordance with the nobility of its nature, *is it free*, when it degrades itself to the level of a trade? A writer naturally must earn money in order to be able to live and write, but under no circumstances must he live and write in order to earn money.

'When Beranger sang:

> *Je ne vis que pour faire des chansons*
> *Si vous o'ôtez ma place Monseigneur,*
> *Je ferai des chansons pour vivre,*

[54] *ibid*, p219
[55] *ibid*, p221

this threat contained an ironic confession that the poet debases himself as soon as poetry becomes for him a means.

'The writer,' continued Marx, 'in no wise considers his work a *means*. It is an *end in itself*, so little is it a means for him and for others that he sacrifices *his* existence to *its* existence, when necessary; and like a religious preacher, in another sense, he applies the principle: "Obey God rather than men" to the men among whom he is himself confined with his human needs and desires. On the other hand I should like to see a tailor from whom I had ordered a Parisian frock-coat bring me a Roman toga, under the pretext that it better fulfils the eternal law of beauty! *The freedom of the press consists primarily in not being a trade.* The writer who degrades it by making it a material means deserves, as punishment for this inner slavery, outer slavery—censorship; or rather his existence is already his punishment.'[56]

Marx's remark about the work of the writer being 'an end in itself' was dictated by his anxiety for the fate of literature, which, freed from the chains of the censor, might fall into the prison of 'bourgeois commercial literary relations' [Lenin]. The point of view expressed by Marx in 1842 had its idealistic side, no doubt. For Marx the struggle against censorship was inseparably bound up with criticism of literary commercialism, and the extolling of revolutionary self-sacrifice was bound up with the preaching of 'creative freedom'. In any event, the entire career of the *Rheinische Zeitung* is proof that Marx was never an exponent of 'art for art's sake' in a trivial sense. This we shall see later.

Not content with subordinating freedom of the press to freedom of trade, the bourgeoisie sought to divide writers into two groups, 'competent' and 'incompetent'. Freedom could be granted only to the former. In this manner the bourgeoisie endeavoured to preserve a greater freedom of

[56] *ibid*, pp222-223

action without destroying class barriers, in fact strengthening them thereby against all unreliable or 'incompetent' persons. They wanted a freedom of the press similar to medieval urban liberties, which were also privileges. 'In such circumstances the press would become a disruptive element instead of a bond uniting the people; class divisions would be reinforced spiritually; and the history of literature would sink to the level of the natural history of separate animal races; disagreements and quarrels could be neither resolved nor avoided; dullness and stupidity would be the rule of the press, because the particular is, I believe, spiritual and free only in conjunction with the whole. Aside from all this, however, inasmuch as *reading* is just as important as *writing*, there must also be *competent* and *incompetent readers*—an inference drawn in Egypt, where the priests, the competent writers, were at the same time the only competent readers.'[57]

It is easy to imagine what 'competence' might come to mean; and we should not be surprised, therefore, that the peasants, as the lowest in the class scale, objected to this discrimination. Marx supported wholeheartedly the plebeian point of view. If limitations of freedom of the press were to exist at all, they should affect the propertied classes as well. 'Everybody is subjected to censorship,' wrote Marx, 'just as under despotism everybody is equalized, not in the sense of respect for personality but in the sense of its depreciation.' Freedom of the press as it was desired by the bourgeoisie could only introduce oligarchy into the realm of the spirit.

Such is the contrast between the plebeian and the bourgeois solution of the problem of freedom of the press. Marx's point of view is quite clear. He wrote: 'When a German looks back upon his history, he finds among the major reasons for his slow political development, as well as for the miserable state of literature before Lessing, the "competent writers". The scholars by profession, by license,

[57] *ibid,* p224

54

and by privilege; the doctors and other asses, the character-less university writers of the seventeenth and eighteenth centuries, with their starched periwigs, their renowned pedantry and their contemptible micrological dissertations, interposed themselves between people and spirit, between life and science, between liberty and man. It was the *incompetent* writers who created our literature. Gottsched or Lessing—choose between them the "competent" writer and the "incompetent" writer!'[58]

[58] *ibid*, pp225-226

8

It is interesting to compare Marx's 'Debates on the Freedom of the Press' [1843][59] with Lenin's 'Party Organization and Party Literature' [1905],[60] in which he speaks of creating a free press, 'free not only in the police sense of the word, but free from Capital as well, free from careerism, free, above all, from anarchic bourgeois individualism'. As opposed to the 'mercenary commercial bourgeois press', and the 'deluded (or hypocritically delusive) dependence' of the bourgeois writer 'upon the money bags, upon bribery, upon patronage', Lenin set up the principle of *party* literature. While Marx's articles in the *Rheinische Zeitung* were on an incomparably lower level of political understanding, there can be no doubt that even in 1842 Marx directed his criticism against not only police censorship but also against freedom of the press in the bourgeois sense.[61] And he also showed, even at this early stage, some signs of the doctrine of party literature.

From the point of view of Marx's political beliefs in 1842, the struggle for party literature coincided with criticism of feudal-bureaucratic censorship. And herein lies the great difference between Lenin's conception of 'party' and that of the young Marx. Lenin held that the destruction of feudal censorship was a problem of the bourgeois-democratic revolution, whereas party literature is a weapon

[59] *ibid*, pp179-229
[60] V I Lenin, *Collected Works*, X, Moscow 1962, pp44-49
[61] 'Comments on the Latest Prussian Censorship Instruction', in Easton and Guddat (eds), *op cit* (footnote 6), pp67-92

of the proletariat in its struggle against anarchic bourgeois literary relations. No doubt the two problems are not separated by a Chinese wall; one grows out of the other. Nevertheless they are different and within certain limits even opposed. To confuse the democratic ideal of a free press with the problem of saving it from the freedom of a 'literary trade' was characteristic of young Marx as a revolutionary democrat.

The censor was his principal opponent. Obeying the dictates of the government, the censor attempted to eradicate every trace of party struggle in literature, prohibiting even the use of party slogans. Already in his first article on freedom of the press, 'Comments on the latest Prussian Censorship Instruction' [1842], Marx unmasked the duplicity of the Prussian government which, while suppressing all party struggle, actually came out as 'one party against another'. The censor's instructions contained some 'aesthetic criticism'. The writer was expected to use a 'serious and modest' style. As a matter of fact, however, any crudeness of style could be forgiven provided the content was acceptable to the government. 'Thus the censor must sometimes judge the content by the form, sometimes the form by the content. First content ceased to serve as a criterion for censorship; and then in turn form vanished.'[62]

The censor's aesthetics imposed on the writer mediocrity on principle. 'The truth is universal. It does not belong to me but to everybody. It possesses me, I do not possess it. My possession is the *form* which constitutes my spiritual individuality. *Le style, c'est l'homme.* And how! The law permits me to write, but on condition that I write in a style not *my own!*'[63] The only legitimate style, according to the royal censorship regulations, was one of vague monotony, a grey official style. 'Voltaire said: *Tous les genres sont bons, excepté le genre ennuyeux* [Every style is good, except the boring style]. Here the *genre ennuyeux*

[62] *ibid,* p90
[63] *ibid,* p71

is the only one permitted.'[64] There is a resemblance between genius and mediocrity. The former is modest, the latter pale. But the modesty of the genius does not mean a renunciation of clarity, conviction, power of expression. 'The essence of the spirit is always *the truth itself*,' wrote Marx. 'And what do you interpret as its essence? *Modesty*. Only a rogue is modest, says Goethe; it is your wish to transform the spirit into such a rogue? Or would you not prefer modesty to be that modesty of genius of which Schiller speaks? Well, then, first transform all your citizens, and above all your censors, into geniuses. In which case the modesty of genius will not, like the language of cultured men, consist in speaking with the accent and employing the dialect which is proper to him; it will consist in forgetting modesty and immodesty, and getting to the bottom of things.'[65]

In this connection Marx's views were not unlike those of Goethe and Hegel on the 'one-sidedness' of genius.[66] Genius, they thought, is marked not by a spineless neutrality to all things, but rather by its definite attitude, its one-sidedness. According to Hegel, the artistic renaissances of the past were bound up with the undeveloped state of social relations, with the artist's dependence upon a solid structure of social life, upon definite contents and traditional forms. The dissolution of this original definiteness Hegel regarded as necessary and progressive. But together with progress and the realization of freedom comes also artistic decadence. 'When the spirit attains a

---

[64] *ibid*, p73

[65] *ibid*, pp72-73

[66] 'Limitation' of aim and work is a recurrent theme in Goethe's *Wilhelm Meisters Wanderjahre*. 'Manysidedness prepares, properly speaking, only the element in which the one-sided can act. . . . The best thing is to restrict oneself.' (Part I, Ch IV), and 'To be acquainted with and to exercise one thing rightly gives higher training than mere halfness in a hundred sorts of things' (Part I, Ch XIII). Cf Part II, Ch XII, and the poem *Natur und Kunst*. For one-sidedness in Hegel see footnote 69 below

consciously adequate and high form, and becomes a free
and pure spirit, art becomes superfluous.'[67] The contemporary 'free' painter [the art of bourgeois society Hegel
calls 'free art'] is deprived of any engrossing content. His
reactions are all automatic, and he knows but a cold devotion to epochs and styles. Everything attracts him,
and nothing in particular. 'Free art' becomes a world
of stylicisms, paraphrases, individual cleverness and
originality.

Young Marx's views have much in common with
this doctrine of Hegel's.

Among Marx's marginal notes on Grund's book we
find the following passage: 'It has been observed that great
men appear in surprising numbers at certain periods
which are invariably characterized by the efflorescence of
art. Whatever the outstanding traits of this efflorescence,
its influence upon men is undeniable; it fills them with its
vivifying force. When this one-sidedness of culture is spent,
mediocrity follows.'[68] As we already know, from his entire
career on the *Rheinische Zeitung*, for example, Marx did
not believe that creative art is irretrievably lost with the
past.

On the contrary, he showed artists the way out of
the crisis which overwhelms art in a society where 'self-
interest' predominates. This way out Marx saw in the
identification of the artist's individuality with a definite
political principle, in the open and vigorously stressed
'accent and dialect' of a political party. It was with this
idea in mind that he attacked the vagueness of romanticism, its flirtations with primitive poetry and modern mysticism, the middle ages and the Orient.

It would not be correct, however, to identify this
viewpoint on the part of Marx with the Hegelian doctrine
of the 'self-limitation' of genius. 'The man who will do
something great,' wrote Hegel, 'must learn, as Goethe says,

[67] G W F Hegel, *The Philosophy of History*, New York 1956
[68] Marginal note in Grund, p25 (see footnote 28 above)—ML

to limit himself. The man who, on the contrary, would do everything, really would do nothing, and fails.'[69] True enough, Hegel criticized the romantics for their aesthetic polytheism, their excessive versatility, their lack of self-limitation. But these ideas Marx interpreted in an entirely different way. 'Self-limitation', as Hegel conceived it, had nothing to do with a revolutionary party and its political principles permeating the creative work of the artist or poet. Quite the contrary, self-limitation must take place within the confines of bourgeois society. In revolution Hegel saw only negative freedom brought about by some 'faction' which, if victorious, becomes another government. Such change, according to Hegel, is only a transitory step towards a better-organized constitutional state, in which every person is a particle in the scheme of the division of labour. Consequently Hegel, contrary to his original plan, justified the 'free art' of bourgeois society in that the artist, after confining himself to a definite theme, must devote himself to its traditional interpretation. Thus bourgeois society, on the very day after the revolution, sought to adopt the 'continuity' and 'certainty' of the old social forms which it had fought as a destructive force. And this was what Hegel had in mind in demanding that the artist becomes conscious of his 'individuality and definite position', and perform his share of work under the protection of a well-organized governmental police.

'Certainty', in the Hegelian sense of the word, by no means conflicts with the 'free art' of bourgeois society, and provides no escape from its false liberty. Only partisanship in art, partisanship in the sense indicated by Marx and Lenin, can give the modern artist that precision and concentration of will, that creative 'one-sidedness' which is essential to genuine art. The beginnings of this doctrine can be found in the creed of young Marx in the period of the *Rheinische Zeitung*.

[69] G W F Hegel, *Logic*, translated by William Wallace, London 1931, p145

9

The *Rheinische Zeitung* was suppressed by the Prussian government early in 1843. At almost the same time Ruge's *Deutsche Jahrbücher* met with a similar fate. The time had come to draw conclusions from the lessons of the 'movement of 1842', when each of the German parties had pursued its own independent course. Marx retired for a time to his 'private study', in order to concentrate on the problems presented by his recent political experiences. These experiences were sufficient to convince young Marx of the inadequacy of the idealist interpretation of history.

While even then, in 1842, Marx's philosophical and political views revealed certain departures from orthodox Hegelianism, nevertheless it was mainly a question of emphasis. His range of interests, as reflected in his sympathies and antipathies, scarcely crossed the boundaries of Hegel's philosophy. 'Self-interest', crude empiricism, the egoism of private interest, still remained Marx's principle objects of attack. Spiritual form was opposed to matter, theory to practice, production (in the spiritual sense) to passive materiality and apathetic consumption. Every social relation was regarded as spiritual, everything material was criticized as a heritage from animal existence. 'In the perfect state,' wrote Marx, 'there is no land ownership, no manufacture, no material things. There are only spiritual forces, while natural forces acquire their place in the state only in their political resurrection and rejuvenation. The State installs spiritual nerves in all nature. It should, therefore, be clear that the ruling force is form and not matter, the nature of the State and not nature outside it, the *"free man"* and not the *"unfree object"*.[70]

Art is the companion of the 'perfect state'. The opposition between art and unfavourable historical conditions is really an eternal antagonism between spirit and nature, between art and material reality. And to remove the fetishistic concretization of human relations, which obstructs the development of art, means to overcome the material foundation of social life. Consequently the struggle against fetishistic conditions is not a struggle between 'flesh and blood', but a struggle against the domination of flesh and blood over man's consciousness. Marx wrote: 'Every subject raised in print, whether favourably or unfavourably, becomes thereby a literary subject, a subject of literary discussion. This is precisely the significance of the press as a mighty lever in the cultural and spiritual enlightenment of the people. It transforms material conflicts into ideal ones, struggles of flesh and blood into spiritual struggles, battles of appetite, greed and practice into battles of theory, reason and form.'[71]

And yet, even in criticizing private property from the standpoint of the 'perfect state', Marx turned against political idealism which ignores the real life of the individual. He embraced Schiller's ideal of man, 'which combines the highest freedom with the fullest existence'. Now this is important. After all, art cannot exist without the senses, and the intellectual content of creative work must be given objective corporeal form.

In the abstract political idea of the citizen free from any material interests, as conceived at the time of the French revolution, art appears as an element of corruption. Rousseau questioned the moral and civic value of art, while the Jacobins denied its aesthetic pleasurability and in painting preferred abstract, almost geometrical allegories.

[70] *Über die standischen Ausschüsse in Preussen* (On the Estates Committees in Prussia), MEGA, I, I/1, p321
[71] *ibid*, p335

C

This disguised a definite class relationship, namely a plebe-ian denial of the 'philosophy of pleasurability', which had been accepted during the eighteenth century by both the nobility and the bourgeoisie.

But this protest against the association of pleasure with culture has an ascetically narrow character. Art was thus menaced by two dangers. On the one hand the Christian-feudal world of the old regime was inimical to it. 'It is obvious that the old regime [France] could give nothing to the poet—neither stimulus to his agile imagin-ation, nor spiritual support.' [Marx's excerpts from Ranke's political history journal.] On the other hand, the abstract democratic ideal of the 'perfect state' (with its formal free-dom and its dualism of political heaven combined with economic empiricism) contains an ascetic disregard of human sensitivity and hence also creative art. We have come across this problem in Marx's Dissertation.

Marx's political and aesthetic problem derived from the whole complex of problems arising out of the bour-geois-democratic revolutions; at the same time it extended beyond these problems. Criticism of private ownership from the standpoint of the 'perfect state' has its conservative side. As an abstract criticism of individual egoism, it applies equally to land-owners, forest-owners, financiers and the oppressed masses, in so far as the latter oppose their right to material well-being—their mass egoism— against the egoism of the privileged classes. This is the reason why such political ideology finds no mass support (witness the indifference of the Parisian workers and paupers to the fall of the Jacobin government). But the Spartan ideal of Rousseau, so revolutionary at the end of eighteenth century, had become clearly reactionary in the hands of Bruno Bauer and his friends, who condemned the 'masses' for their devotion to material interests. Similarly Rousseau's negation of art, as something that cannot be separated from purely material problems of existence, had become reactionary. And indeed the problem of the histor-ical rights of art does stand behind the question of the masses' right to improvement of their sensuous material existence.

The first burning lesson which Marx learned from the suppression of the *Rheinische Zeitung* was that it was necessary, first of all, to do away with the old doctrine of the sinfulness of the flesh, whether in its Christian-feudal, idealist-ancient, romantic, or classical form.

Thus it was necessary to pass from the abstract to the concrete, from the 'ideals of 1793' to 'flesh and blood'. But how was this to be accomplished? At that stage of the German revolution, two roads were open. The first had been chosen by the great social thinkers of the preceding period; it can be described as the road of 'reconciliation'. Schiller, for instance, sought to combine the spiritual with the sensuous, to reconcile the revolutionary 'citizen' with the egotistic bourgeois. In the concept of the 'Aesthetic State', he resolved the contradiction between the 'State of Absence of Determination or Empty Infiniteness' [*Bestimmbarkeit*] and the 'Determinate State' [*Bestimmung*]. Each of these contradictory aspects, taken in isolation, is inimical to aestheticism. Material life is dominated by greed and conflicting interests. Ideal life, in demanding self-sacrifice, is too severe to yield happiness. The problem is how to unite idea with sensory form, spiritual life with corporeal existence. This problem was resolved in Schiller's 'Aesthetic State'.[72]

Hegel, too, followed essentially the same road. He comprehended quite correctly the abstract character of revolutionary self-consciousness of—Fichte's 'Ego = Ego' and French '*égalité*'. However, the transition from the abstract to the concrete he interpreted not as a continuous revolutionary process in which the citizens become differentiated and class interests concretized, but on the contrary, as an advance from the turbulence of the cosmic spirit in its 'years of discipleship' to bold reconciliation with reality.

[72] Friedrich Schiller, *Letters on the Aesthetic Education of Man*, especially Letters XIX and XX, in *Works of Friedrich Schiller* (Cambridge edition), VIII, pp5-126

Hegel's cosmic spirit goes through all the successive stages of the post-revolutionary 'transitory period' of bourgeois society—from Thermidor to constitutional monarchy. True enough, he subjects bourgeois society to sharp criticism; but not in its historically determined form—rather as the material aspect of a society *par excellence*. This negation is next declared to be abstract and in its transition from the abstract to the concrete is declared to be a return to material, sensuous existence, i.e. to bourgeois society— with this difference, however, that the prosaic and sordid character of bourgeois relations here acquires a deep mystical significance as the embodiment of the active essence of the spirit. Such, briefly, is the meaning of the 'speculative methods' of German idealist philosophy.

This is particularly clear in the field of aesthetics. Hegel, with remarkable insight, points out the contradictoriness of the historical development of art and society. But this historically conditioned phenomenon he regards as an inevitable process in the liberation of the spirit from the senses. Artistic creation disappears along with local and national limitations, along with the feudal-patriarchal order. Under contemporary relationships, under the latest political and educational institutions, it is just as out of place as the boasting and figurative language of the heroic epoch, where dry clarity of exposition and ability to think abstractedly were required. The Universal Spirit of bourgeois society makes the sensuous concrete world of art an anachronism.

As we already know, Hegel does not stop at this stage of logical development. In aesthetics, too, he seeks a way to the concrete. Art, repudiated by historical progress, is reborn in his imagination, but already as modern 'free' art. If bourgeois society can have its kings and priests, why not its own art? Like Adam Smith, Hegel declares the 'servants of the muses' to be *non-productive workers*, in order to recognize their right to serve. Art as a *sensuous* phenomenon thus acquires its right to existence in so far as it is reconciled as a *spiritual* phenomenon with existing 'sensuous reality', that is to say, with the prosaic nature of bourgeois social relations. For instance, Hegel points out that the portrayal of anything prosaic and accidental assumes a great significance in modern art. Thus he is won by the ability of the Dutch to make attractive even the most prosaic and vulgar scenes. According to Hegel, this reconciliation with life is what constitutes, in the main, the transition from the abstract to the concrete.

As one who lived at a time when the proletariat had not yet appeared on the historical scene, Hegel saw the road from the abstract to the concrete merely in the reconciliation of the childishly glorified 'citizen' with the sober and prosaic 'bourgeois'. Hence the 'years of discipleship' were understood not as revolutionary experience, but as 'experience' in the vulgar sense, as the abandonment of revolutionary impulses.

Marx followed an entirely different road.

Realizing how abstract was any criticism of social relations from the standpoint of the 'perfect state', Marx sought an approach to concrete reality. The experience of 1842 convinced him that the only solution of the contradiction between economic necessity and formal political freedom lies in the elimination of this contradiction, that is, in the abolition of the premise of private property. The only social force capable of solving this problem is the proletariat, the class representing the 'decomposition of the previous world order'. Marx's prophetic recognition of the historical role of the proletariat appears for the first time at the end of 1843 and the beginning of 1844, following a thorough study of French and English political literature. The doctrine of the historical role of the working class was evolved as a way out of the various contradictions of Hegelian philosophy, with its approval of bourgeois society and its view of the State as the ultimate goal of historical development. 'When the proletariat proclaims the *dissolution of the existing order of things*,' wrote Marx, 'it is merely announcing the *secret of its own existence*, for it is in itself the virtual dissolution of this order of things.

When the proletariat *desires the negation of private property,* it is merely elevating to a *general principle* of society what it already involuntarily embodies in itself as the negative product of society. . . . Just as philosophy finds in the proletariat its *material* weapons, so the proletariat finds in philosophy its *spiritual* weapons.'[73]

This turn of thought was also reflected in Marx's aesthetic beliefs.

[73] 'Contribution to the Critique of Hegel's Philosophy of Right. Introduction', in T B Bottomore (ed), *Karl Marx: Early Writings,* London 1963, pp58-59

10

A detailed criticism of speculative aesthetics is to be found in *The Holy Family*, which Marx and Engels wrote in opposition to their former friends, Bruno Bauer and his group. The greater part of this book is devoted to a discussion of an article on Eugène Sue's *The Mysteries of Paris* written by the Left Hegelian Szeliga. In addition to criticizing Szeliga, however, Marx subjects to a devastating analysis not only Sue's novel but also the entire moral and aesthetic creed of the 'dominant personality' of the nineteenth century—the bourgeois.

The Mysteries of Paris, that 'European Scheherazade', as Belinsky called it, enjoyed a tremendous success in the forties of the last century. Flirting with social problems and offering hypocritically moral solutions, Sue had become exceedingly popular throughout Europe.

Among Sue's admirers were the Bauer brothers, at that time publishers of the *Allgemeine Literaturzeitung* in Berlin. Through Szeliga, this literary journal had announced that Sue's solution of the social problem accorded with their speculative solution. Marx, by comparing *The Mysteries of Paris* with Szeliga's critical interpretation of it, proved conclusively that the actual contents of the novel had clearly been distorted in order to suit the purposes of 'critical criticism' and its speculative assumptions. That an analogy existed between the speculative method and the spirit of bourgeois romanticism, Marx made no attempt to deny. Quite the contrary, he proved, ironically, that the 'mystery of speculative construction' and *The Mysteries of*

Paris had one and the same ideological basis. He said:
'Just as for Rodolphe all men hold the standpoint of good
and bad and are judged according to these two fixed concepts, so for Herr Bauer and consorts, men hold the standpoint of either the critics or the masses. But both transform
real men into *abstract standpoints*.'[74]

The Holy Family contains a classic section on 'The
Mystery of Speculative Construction',[75] in which Marx
shows that Hegel's method, the root of all the discoveries
of 'critical criticism', is based on idealistic mystification.
The philosopher constructs out of numerous real entities
an abstract notion which he calls substance (for instance,
'fruit' is the substance of the pear, the apple, the almond,
etc.) From the idealist point of view, this notion has real,
absolute existence, whereas the various concrete entities are
mere semblances, modes of existence of the fruit. The dissolution of material existence in the general concept is,
however, a mere abstraction. Recognizing this deficiency,
the idealist attempts to renounce abstraction, but he does
so in a 'speculative, mystical manner'. He converts the
abstraction into an active spiritual essence generating multi-
form varieties of concrete, earthly realities.

The methods of speculative aesthetics are built around
this idealistic sleight-of-hand. 'It has been necessary to
make these preliminary remarks,' wrote Marx, 'in order to
render Herr Szeliga intelligible. Until now Herr Szeliga had
included realities, such as law and civilization, in the category of mystery and has thus made a "mystery" of substance. But it is only now that he rises to *Hegelian* speculative heights, and transforms the "mystery" into an independent subject *embodying* real conditions and persons,
and manifesting itself in countesses, marquis, grisettes, por-
ters, notaries and charlatans, as well as amorous intrigues,
balls, doors, etc. After having constructed out of the real

[74] Karl Marx and Friedrich Engels, *The Holy Family or
Critique of Critical Critique*, Moscow 1956, pp255-256
[75] *ibid*, Ch V, Sec 2, pp78-83 (also in Easton and Guddat
op cit (footnote 6), pp369-374)

world the category of "mystery", he constructs out of this category the real world.'[76] And this is done not only by Szeliga in his literary criticism; the author of *The Mysteries of Paris* does the very same thing. He converts living characters into mere allegorical figures. 'Eugène Sue's characters [Chourineur and The Schoolmaster] are made to expound as their own ideas, as the conscious motives of their acts, the literary intentions which caused the author to make them act in such and such a way. They constantly say: In this respect I have improved, or in that other, or again in that other, etc. Since they do not lead a real, full life, they must by their language lend colour to their insignificant characteristics.'[77] This criticism of speculative literary interpretation holds true to this very day.

As opposed to the idealistic subordination of the concrete to the abstract, Marx stood for the self-development of living forces and characters. In real, sensuous experience the 'where' and the 'whence' cannot be known in advance. Idealistic philosophy does not take this attitude, however; rather it holds that everything is permeated with teleology and exists for a purpose, while the individual is merely the voice of some developing idea. Not content with criticizing idealistic aesthetics and hypocritical idealistic literature, Marx went on to arraign that 'condition of the world' which makes the individual a mere tool of blind social forces, and which is thus diametrically opposed to the 'epic condition of the world' described in Hegelian aesthetics. Szeliga's attempts to portray nineteenth-century Paris as the background for an epos, and Sue's complicated plot as an 'epic event', could evoke only sarcasm on the part of Marx.

The hypocritical Sue attempted to solve the dialectics of good and evil by means of an abstract assertion of nobility and honesty; but his critic Marx sided with those characters in *The Mysteries of Paris* who admit that they stand in direct opposition to honesty and other virtues of

[76] *ibid*, p82
[77] *ibid*, p242

'decent society', such as the butcher Chourineur, Fleur-de-Marie, The Schoolmaster, Rigolette, and other characters representing the unofficial side of the civilized world. In discussing them Marx departed but little from Hegel.

'Nobility' and 'baseness' are interfusing categories, as we know. For the 'enlightened', 'what is characterized as good is bad, and vice versa'.[78] A high evaluation of the 'base', 'disgraceful', 'disintegrated' consciousness is one of the best features of Hegel's *Phenomenology of Mind*, wherein he discusses those social groups which represent the negative side of social progress. These groups are marked by poverty, disintegration of family life, contempt for the moral rules of 'good' people. However, by virtue of the dialectics of the historical process, these 'bad' and 'base' people—as 'enlightened' society designates them—turn out to be truly good and noble. This analysis gave Hegel a deep insight into the dualism of progress into the relativity of 'nobility' and 'baseness' and the hypocrisy of bourgeois society, where, as Mandeville had shown, individual vices become public virtues. In so far as they perceive the 'subhuman' character of their mode of existence, and the contradictoriness of social relations, these people rise above official society, which merely seeks its own interest under the false guise of nobility and honesty. While the 'noble', 'good' people live in a world of abstract opposition between good and bad, other people—such as Rameau's nephew—represent the dialectics of history, which they instinctively comprehend. Hegel also refers to *Rameau's Nephew*.

It is interesting to note that this little masterpiece from the pen of the great Encyclopaedist was among the literary works most prized by Marx. Diderot was his favourite prose writer. In 1869 he sent a copy of *Rameau's Nephew* to Engels, with the following quotation from Hegel: 'The mocking laughter at existence, at the confusion of the whole and at itself, is the disintegrated con-

78 G W F Hegel, *The Phenomenology of Mind*, New York 1931, p526

sciousness, aware of itself and expressing itself, and is at the same time the last audible echo of all this confusion. . . . It is the self-disintegrating nature of all relations and their conscious disintegration. . . . In this aspect of the return to self the *vanity of all things* is the self's *own vanity,* or the self is itself vanity . . . but as the indignant consciousness it is aware of its own disintegration and by that knowledge has immediately transcended it. . . . Every part of this world either gets its mind expressed here or is spoken of intellectually and declared for what it is. The *honest consciousness* (the role which Diderot allots to himself in the dialogue) takes each element for a permanent entity and does not realize in its uneducated thoughtlessness that it is doing just the opposite. But the disintegrated consciousness is the consciousness of reversal and indeed of absolute reversal; its dominating element is the concept, which draws together the thoughts that to the honest consciousness lie so wide apart: hence the brilliance of its language. Thus the contents of the mind's speech about itself consist in the reversal of all conceptions and realities; the universal deception of oneself and others and the shamelessness of declaring this deception is therefore precisely the greatest truth. . . . To the quiet consciousness, which in its honest way goes on singing the melody of the True and the Good in even tones, i.e. on one note, this speech appears as "a farrago of wisdom and madness".[79]

Hegel, whom we cannot place on the same level with Szeliga and Bauer, was able to interpret classical works of literature; but what was possible to Hegel was unthinkable in representatives of the French bourgeoisie of the period of Louis Philippe:

'More amusing than Hegel's commentary is that of M. Jules Janin, from which you will find extracts in the appendix to the little volume. This *cardinal de la mer* [sea-cardinal] feels the lack of a moral in Diderot's *Rameau* and has therefore set the thing right by the discovery

[79] Marx, letter to Engels, 15 April 1869, *Selected Correspondence,* edited by Dona Torr, London 1934, p260

that all Rameau's contrariness arises from his vexation at not being a "born gentleman". The Kotzebue-ish rubbish which he has piled up on this cornerstone is being performed as a melodrama in London. From Diderot to Jules Janin is no doubt what the physiologists call regressive metamorphosis. The French intellect as it was *before* the revolution and *under Louis Philippe!* . . .'[80]

Thus according to Hegel the 'disintegrated' consciousness becomes its own opposite in so far as it recognizes itself to be a product of the decomposition of the old world order. It perceives the hypocrisy and falsity of all social relations and becomes the 'indignant consciousness'. These words of Hegel concerning the 'indignant consciousness' have a particular bearing upon the lumpen-proletariat —'the mass existence of which, after the decay of the middle ages, preceded the mass appearance of the *secular* proletariat'[81]—and particularly upon the proletariat of the nineteenth century. 'In the fully developed proletariat everything human, everything even resembling the human, approaches the vanishing point; in the conditions of existence of the proletariat all the conditions of existence of present-day society are converged to their most inhuman focus; there man has lost his identity, but at the same time he has not only acquired the theoretical consciousness of this loss, he has been driven, out of distress no longer to be *evaded*, no longer to be ameliorated, utterly imperious —as the practical expression of necessity—to revolt against this inhumanity: therefore the proletariat can and must free itself. It cannot free itself, however, without doing away with its conditions of existence. And it cannot do away with these conditions without doing away with *all* the inhuman conditions of existence of present-day society which are converged in its situation.'[82] Socialist writers do not regard the proletarians as gods, but they know that the

[80] *ibid*, pp260-261
[81] Karl Marx and Friedrich Engels, *The German Ideology*, London 1965, p216
[82] *The Holy Family*, Moscow 1956, p52

social position of the proletariat dictates its historical task; and furthermore that 'a large part of the English and French proletariat have already become conscious of their historical role and are making unceasing efforts to give to this consciousness the utmost clarity.'[83]

In *The German Ideology*, Marx assails Stirner's ridicule of the proletariat, and describes the worker as the human counterpart of the sane and selfish representatives of 'decent society'. The 'passion' of the proletarian stands far above the 'worry' of the bourgeois. Even in Sue's portrayal, the lowest plebeian-proletarian is far nobler and more humane than those who take it upon themselves to correct his faults. Consider, for instance, Rigolette of *The Mysteries of Paris*. 'In her Eugène Sue portrayed that admirable, human character, the Parisian grisette. However, out of his devotion to the bourgeoisie and his own transcendentalism, he was forced to idealize her from a moral standpoint. He had to extenuate the salient trait of Rigolette's character and situation: her disdain of marriage, her naïve relations with the student and the worker. Yet it is precisely these naïve relations which place her in truly human contrast with the hypocritical, avaricious, egoistical bourgeois wife, and the entire bourgeois world, that is to say, the entire official world.'[84]

Needless to say, the author of *The Mysteries of Paris* was far from portraying the transition from 'indignant consciousness' to revolutionary consciousness. On the contrary, because of the novel's structure every strong and beautiful character is made to develop in the opposite direction, or at least is interrupted in the normal development of his nature. In this fact Marx saw two characteristics of the literature of bourgeois apologists: first, its idealistic attitude towards the reality portrayed, resulting in the transformation of every living character into an automaton designed to prove the author's abstract ideas; and second, its idealistic ethics, which hypocritically rejects sensuousness only to re-

[83] *ibid*, p53
[84] *ibid*, p102

admit it in a more 'de-humanized' form. The self-development of sensuous, concrete reality, or its subordination to an alien force: fight or submission: such, in the final analysis is the fundamental distinction between the aesthetic-philosophical ideas of Marx and those of Szeliga and Sue.

Materialist dialectics, as founded by Marx, is grounded in historical reality with all its contradictions and contrasts. The solution of all these contradictions it seeks neither in a speculative 'Supreme Unity', nor in the restraint of the centrifugal forces of actuality, but rather in the full development of these contradictions and antagonisms. Marx's doctrine of the historical role of the proletariat holds that this class 'is not a mass of humanity mechanically bowed down under the weight of society, but a mass originating out of decay', and hence it becomes a revolutionary constructive force which in its turn negates '*all* the inhuman conditions of existence of present-day society'.[85]

Idealist dialectics, whether presented in Hegel's classic form or in Szeliga's vulgar and sentimental form, is the very opposite of this method. Its philosophical formula consists in a reconciliation of motion with rest, stability with disorganization, general relativity with common sense. It finds the unity of opposites not in the consecutive development of contradictions but in their defeat—in the curdling of the revolutionary process. Thus Hegel believed that 'indignant consciousness', revolution and reign of terror are succeeded by the reign of 'morality', in which the 'self-conscious Spirit' solves the contradictions of the epoch of 'enlightenment'.

Like other German philosophers of the eighteenth century, Hegel employed such terms as 'the mob' and 'the common people' to describe the workers. Although he criticized the rich and defended the poor, his praises of the aesthetic aspect of poverty carried no revolutionary implications. In admiring Murillo's beggar-boys, for instance, Hegel regarded as beautiful their jolly satisfaction with their lot, their carefree indolence rendering them the equal

[85] *ibid*, p52

of the gods. Like those fairy tales of happy beggars and
unhappy millionaires, quite common in eighteenth-century
literature, this delight in poverty had an obvious touch of
banality.

Marx's attitude was quite different. *The Mysteries of
Paris* deals with various types of the lumpen-proletariat;
but even in these sunken representatives of a great class,
Marx found many traits far more deserving of the artist's
attention than the prosaic monotony of bourgeois relations.
Marx considered virile determination, fighting ability and
strength of character—traits inherent in characters like
Chourineur, The Schoolmaster, Fleur-de-Marie, etc.—to
be among the best subjects for artistic treatment. And he
not merely pointed out that plebeian-proletarian types
are fit subjects for literary treatment; he actually spoke of
literature as originating in the *'lower classes of the people'*
(Bauer's term).

'If', wrote Marx, in opposition to Bauer, '*the* critics
were better acquainted with the movement of the lower
classes of the people [here Marx referred to the proletarian
movement], they would know that the enormous obstacles
which these people meet in practical life change them every
day. The new literature in prose and in poetry which is
coming from the lower classes of England and France
would prove to them that the lower classes of the people
are quite capable of rising spiritually without the *blessing*
of the *Holy Spirit* of *critical criticism*.'[86]

This will suffice to indicate Marx's attitude toward
the problem of proletarian literature. As the working class,
in the process of its revolutionary reconstruction of the
world, reconstructs its own nature, it produces its own
literature—upon a level incomparably higher than the
literature of bourgeois apologists.

[86] *ibid*, p181

11

'Only the philosophical materialism of Marx,' wrote Lenin, 'has shown the proletariat a way out of the spiritual slavery in which all the oppressed classes have stagnated till now.' Conversely, it was their very recognition of the historical role of the proletariat which served Marx and Engels as the transition to the theory of dialectical materialism. From the height which they attained, the founders of Marxism could subject to devastating criticism all 'German ideology', that is, the idealist school of philosophy plus the various forms of petty bourgeois socialism and anarchism connected with it.

As we have already seen, Marx's criticism of Hegelian aesthetics was to some extent self-criticism as well. If hitherto he had considered the material side of society to be lower in the scale of importance, now the scales were practically reversed: the lowest became the *foundation* of the entire superstructure. The development of all aspects of social reality is determined, in the final analysis, by the *self-development* of material production and re-production. Accordingly, the role of creative art is regarded differently. Art, like law or the state, for example, has no independent history, i.e. outside the brains of ideologists. In reality, literature and art are conditioned by the entire historical development of society.

It does not follow from this, of course, that, according to the theory of dialectical materialism, art plays merely a secondary role (as Pisarev would have it, in putting a shoemaker above Raphael). On the contrary, it is the idealist *exaltation* of art over material reality which results in the ascetic *debasement* of art to the level of its mere sensuous relationship to life. Whereas Hegel ascribed the decadence of art to its sensuous nature, Marx explained this phenomenon in terms of unfavourable historical circumstances, and defended the rights of art, the rights of sensuousness as such. In this respect he was influenced by Feuerbach.

In its social implication, Feuerbach's aesthetic-philosophical ideal was 'progressive bourgeois democracy or revolutionary democracy' [Lenin]. Feuerbach defended the rights of the flesh, in opposition to the speculative doctrine of the relative worthlessness of sensuous existence, and the implied subjugation of 'oppressed creatures' to their oppressors. According to Hegel, since the material-sensuous always produces an 'alienation' [*Entfremdung*] of the spirit, 'assimilation' [*Aneignung*] of the world of things is possible only through cognition [*Erkenntnis*]. Art is an imperfect form of cognition. Against this concept, which dissolves art in abstract thought, Feuerbach justly launched his criticism. Man makes the world his own not by means of the reasoning faculties alone, but through the use of all his powers.

We find analogous thoughts in Marx. For instance: 'Man asserts himself in the material world not only by means of thought, but also by means of all his senses.' The transition from idealism to materialism is inevitably bound up with the emancipation of art, as a sensuous form of consciousness, from slavish subordination to abstract thought. In his introduction to the *Critique of Political Economy*, Marx distinguishes between the 'artistic-religious-practical-spiritual assimilation of the world' and its assimilation by means of 'a thinking mind'.[87]

However, in rejecting the Hegelian conception of history as a constant struggle between spirit and matter, Feuerbach also rejected both the concept of contradiction and the concept of historical 'intervention' [*Vermittlung*].

[87] Karl Marx, *A Contribution to the Critique of Political Economy*, London 1971, pp205ff

He considered the assimilation of the world to be a purely contemplative process, whereas even the idealist Hegel regarded it as an activity, even if an activity of pure reason, of 'abstract spiritual labour'. Hence Feuerbach's suave apologetics of 'man' (in his harmony with 'nature'), which underlay all the literature of German 'true socialism'. The humanistic aesthetics of Feuerbach and Grün in the final analysis amounted to an embellishment of the worker's plight in bourgeois society. The only thing required of 'man' was that he become aware of his unity with the surrounding world and declare it his *own*, even though he is in fact surrounded by the 'alien' [*Fremdes*]. The task of critically annihilating German 'true socialism'—'in verse and prose'—fell to Engels.[88]

With Marx and Engels, 'assimilation' acquired an historical character. Rejecting the idealistic conception of the sensuous-material world as an 'alienation' of the spirit, Marx knew full well that this world becomes man's 'own' not by virtue of the human capacity for contemplation, but only after lasting struggle. The 'objectification' of reality, the modification of its crude natural form, is itself a material process, a process of 'projecting' man's subjective forces and abilities. 'The history of industry and the concrete existence of industry are the open book of fundamental human forces, human psychology in sensuous form.'[89]

The senses have their own history. Neither the object of art nor the subject capable of aesthetic experience comes of itself—these arise out of the process of man's creative activity. 'Only music awakens the musical sensibility of man . . . for the unmusical ear the most beautiful music means nothing . . . and so the sensibilities of the social man are different from those of the non-social man. Only through tne objective development of the richness of

[88] See especially *Deutscher Sozialismus in Versen und Prosa* and *Die wahren Sozialisten*, MEGA, I, 6, pp33-71 and 73-116
[89] 'Economic and Philosophical Manuscripts' in T B Bottomore (ed), *Karl Marx: Early Writings*, London 1963, p162

human nature is the richness of subjective human sensibility—the ear for music, the eye for beauty of form, in
short, sensibilities capable of human enjoyment, sensibilities which manifest themselves as human powers—in part
evolved, in part created. . . . The objectification of human
nature both in theory and in practice was necessary, therefore, both in order to humanize man's sensibility and to
create for all the richness of human and natural existence
a corresponding human sensibility.'[90] The aesthetic impulse
is not something biologically inherent, something preceding
social development. It is a historical product, the result of
a long series of material and intellectual production. 'The
object of art,' wrote Marx, 'as well as any other product,
creates an artistic and beauty-enjoying public. Production
thus produces not only an object for the individual, but
also an individual for the object.'[91]

Originally production and consumption were determined by animal nature. Work was instinctive. Consumption was carried out in a brutal, predatory manner. 'The
animal,' wrote Marx, 'is inseparably one with its life
activity. There is no distinction between the two; they are
identical. Man makes his life-activity the object of his
desire and his consciousness. He possesses conscious life-
activity. It is not a fixed necessity to which he is inextric-
ably bound. Conscious life-activity immediately distinguishes human from animal life-activity.'[92] 'A spider', said
Marx in *Capital*, 'conducts operations that resemble those
of a weaver, and a bee puts to shame many an architect
in the construction of her cells. But what distinguishes
the worst architect from the best of bees is this, that the
architect raises his structure in imagination before he
erects it in reality.'[93] Where does man derive this ability?

[90] *ibid,* pp161-162
[91] *A Contribution to the Critique of Political Economy,*
London 1971, p197
[92] 'Economic and Philosophical Manuscripts', in T B Bottomore (ed), *Karl Marx: Early Writings,* London 1963, p127
[93] *Capital,* I, Moscow 1959, p178

Schiller, in his famous poem, *Die Küntsler*, says:

Im Fliess kann dich die Beine meistern,
In der Geschicklichkeit ein Wurm dein Lehrer sein,
Dein Wissen theilest du mit vorgezognen Geistern,
Die Kunst, o Mensch, hast du allein.[94]

Kant and Schiller clearly expressed that old idealist dogma that man from the very beginning belongs to two worlds: spiritual and sensuous. Art is the middle turn in the universal hierarchy rising from the savage beast to the incorporeal inhabitant of the ether. The contradiction between the spiritual and the sensuous thus acquires a pre-historical character.

The formation of consciousness and perceptivity out of instinctive life was a phenomenon of historical development. They did not exist from the very beginning, but came into being in the process of growing productive activity. Consciousness is the very opposite of material things, yet it is identical with them. Man 'opposes himself to Nature as one of her own forces, setting in motion arms and legs, head and hands, the natural forces of his body, in order to appropriate Nature's productions in a form adapted to his own wants. By thus acting on the external world and changing it, he at the same time changes his own nature. He develops his slumbering powers and compels them to act in obedience to his sway.'[95] He realizes a purpose of his own that 'gives the law to his modus operandi'. And to this purpose he subordinates his will also. This subordination, continued Marx, is not a single act. 'Besides the exertion of the bodily organs, the process demands that during the whole operation, the workman's will be steadily in consonance with his purpose. This means

[94] *Schillers Sämtliche Werke*, I, Stuttgart 1862, p82
In industry, the bee a palm may bear;
In skill, the worm a lesson may impart;
With spirits blest thy knowledge thou dost share;
But thou, O man, alone hast art!

[95] *Capital*, I, Moscow 1959, p177

close attention. The less he is attracted by the nature of the work, and the mode in which it is carried on, and the less, therefore, he enjoys it as something which gives play to his bodily and mental powers, the more close his attention is forced to be.'[96]

Thus the distinction between physical and mental powers is identified with the need of conscious labour. This distinction does not always take the form of inimical relationships, however. Only where the worker derives no satisfaction from his work, only where the will and the attention must overcome instinctive repugnance, only there begins the Kantian opposition between work and play. This inimical relationship between the senses and reason, between the poetical play of fantasy and the prose of life —a relationship raised by idealist aesthetics to the level of a fatal division of the human spirit—has its foundation in definite forms of production. As we shall see later, it attains its highest development in the capitalistic structure of life.

Thus, with the appearance of conscious labour out of purely natural functions, with the liberation from natural limitations, grows also the unity of man and nature. We set conscious goals before ourselves, which are realized through practice in the objective world. Thus the process of humanizing the world. This is possible, Marx said, only in so far as 'the object becomes for him [man] a social object and he himself a social being, just as society becomes for him a being in that object'. In contradistinction to animals, man produces not only consciously but also collectively. His group life consists not in given instinctive functions, but in *social production*.

'The practical production of the *world of objects* and the *modification* of inorganic nature is proof that man is a conscious member of the species, that is, a creature who considers the species to be related to himself, and himself related to the species. True enough, the animal also

[96] *ibid*, p178

produces; it builds its nest or its dwelling, like the bee, the beaver, the ant, etc. The animal, however, produces only that which it immediately needs for itself or its offspring. The production of the animal is particular, that of man, universal; the animal produces only under the pressure of direct physical necessity, whereas man produces even when free from physical necessity and does not really produce until such necessity is absent; the animal produces only itself, while man reproduces all nature; the product of the animal is directly related to its physical body, while man transcends his product. The animal creates according to the measure and need of the species to which it belongs, while man can produce according to the measure of every species, he can apply the proper measure to each case. Man, therefore, can also create according to the laws of beauty.'[97]

Artistic modification of the world of things is, therefore, one of the ways of assimilating nature. Creative activity is merely one instance of the realization of an idea or a purpose in the material world; it is a process of object-ification. But as distinct from the immediate, crude form of assimilation, art begins only where a general measure lies at the basis of theoretical activity, or, more simply, where objects and their images in the human brain are not distorted by interference on the part of outside forces, where the artist makes his medium speak its own language, thus revealing its inner truth. An aesthetic relation to reality is one of inner organic unity with the object, equally as remote from abstract, contemplative harmony with it as from arbitrary distortion of its own dialectic. In such a form, this unity by no means contradicts the progressive development of social production; quite the contrary, it is its highest spiritual attainment.

Though the passage quoted above [written in 1844] still reflects the terminology of Feuerbach, it already gives evidence of the distinctive character of Marx's materialism,

[97] 'Economic and Philosophical Manuscripts', in T B Bottomore (ed) *Karl Marx: Early Writings*, London 1963, pp127-128

namely the idea of *productive* sensuous and practical activity, the primacy of production over consumption. Whereas Feuerbach, whenever he dealt with the subject of art, always started with contemplation, Marx invariably stressed the significance of the productive factor, which determines aesthetic needs and evolves them, through practice, out of their initial crudeness. Aesthetic desire, and the aesthetically developed individual, are not born of some teleological supermaterial power, they are formed by the self-development of social life, in which real empirical man rises above the limitations imposed by circumstances. Marx abstracted from Vischer's *Aesthetik* the following interesting remark: 'That the enjoyment of the beautiful is immediate, and that it requires education would seem to be contradictory. But man becomes what he is and arrives at his own true nature only through education.'

And so, with the development of objective activity, i.e. material production, our abilities also are developed. 'Consumption emerges from its first stage of natural crudeness', and in its turn influences and perfects production, 'by bringing to a state of readiness, through the necessity of repetition, the disposition to produce developed in the first act of production'.[98] Such is also the dialectical solution of the problem of the subjective and the objective in creative art and in the aesthetic attitude toward reality. Here, just as in the materialist theory of cognition, the point is not in abstract relations, but in historical development. The main thing is the transition from the inartistic to the artistic, the gradual development of man's creative abilities and understanding by means of spiritual production itself, and, moreover, by means of the expansion of the 'objective world' of industry. The stone axe, the clay pot, the keyboard instrument, are landmarks in the development of man's visual perception, musical sense and artistic appreciation in general.

However, the means and the objects of production

[98] *A Contribution to the Critique of Political Economy*, London 1971, pp197-198

are inseparably connected with definite historical forms of society. And this fact makes infinitely more complicated the dialectical history of art in its relation to material production.

12

At a first glance it might appear that from the Marxist standpoint the development of the material productive forces of society parallels artistic development: the higher the general state of production, the greater and richer the art. This solution of the problem has been advanced by many writers dealing with the Marxist conception of the history of art. But this interpretation suffers from abstraction and is, therefore, erroneous.

Marx himself expressed his point of view with sufficient clarity in his introduction to the *Critique of Political Economy*. He speaks there of the unequal relation between the development of material production and art: 'It is well known that certain periods of highest development of art stand in no direct connection with the general development of society, nor with the material basis and the skeleton structure of its organization. Witness the example of the Greeks as compared with the modern nations or even Shakespeare.'[99] The attitude towards nature underlying Greek mythology and art is totally incompatible with Roberts & Co. or the Crédit Mobilier. 'Is Achilles possible side by side with powder and lead? Or is the *Iliad* at all compatible with the printing press and steam press? Does not singing and reciting and the muses necessarily go out of existence with the appearance of the printer's bar, and do not, therefore, disappear the prerequisities of epic poetry?'[100]

[99] *ibid*, p215
[100] *ibid*, p216

This constantly misinterpreted passage seems to contradict the materialist conception of history. Either art develops coincidentally with the growth of the productive forces of society, in which case one can indeed speak of the Marxist conception of the history of art, or there is no connection between the two, in which case it is impossible to apply historical materialism to art. Generally speaking, this is how the problem is often presented. However, to put it thus means to misunderstand the basic theory of historical materialism. As we shall see in a moment, the doctrine of the historically-conditioned contradiction between art and society is as indispensable an element of the Marxist interpretation of the history of art as is the doctrine of their unity.

The formation and development of human needs is a process which does not proceed uniformly with the historical process of 'assimilating' the world of things. The world is 'assimilated' by means of the 'alienation' of human forces; together with the increase of freedom grows the strength of natural necessity. This paradox of progress was noted long ago by philosophers too numerous to mention.

In the philosophy of Hegel this notable fact of world history received its most abstract expression. Historical development, said Hegel, is not a harmonious ascent, but rather 'a cruel repugnant labour against oneself'. The spirit —Hegel's 'demi-urge, the creator of reality'—is in a state of constant inner struggle. It realizes itself through contradiction with, and alienation from, itself. Periods of happiness, therefore, are empty pages of history, and progress is inseparable from decay in whole fields of human endeavour. Such, for instance, is the fate of art, in which the spirit contemplates its own essence in an inadequate form.

But only in the theory of dialectical materialism, the ideological expression of the proletariat's communist revolution, does this problem of the non-uniformity of progress acquire an historical character. For Marx 'alienation' characterized not the sensuous-material world in general, but only one specific historical phase—the fetishistic world of commodity production. ('Selling is the practice of alienation.'[101]) Only in Marxism, therefore, is the question of the historical destiny of art scientifically stated and solved.

The doctrine of the non-uniformity of historical development is first stated in *The German Ideology* (1845-46) of Marx and Engels. In the magnificent first part of this work, history is presented as a process of formation and development of antagonisms whose origins go back to pre-historical times and whose only solution lies in the communist revolution of the working class. 'The prehistoric stage of human society' is a story of division of labour, separation of town and country, etc. 'The division of labour does not become an actual division until the division of material and spiritual work appears. . . . Together with the *division of labour* is given the possibility, nay, the actuality, that spiritual activity and material activity, pleasure and work, production and consumption, will fall to the lot of different individuals.'[102] This phenomenon establishes a definite contradiction between the three elements (*Momenten*) of the social process: 'productive forces', 'social relations' and 'consciousness'. These 'can and must enter into contradiction with each other', and the only solution of these contradictions is: 'that the division of labour be again abolished'.

The division of labour has, however, two aspects and two historical forms. Of the numerous writers and social thinkers of the eighteenth century who described the pauperizing effects of the division of labour, none ever doubted that in its early stages this division actually promoted individual inclinations and talents, thus functioning quite differently from that man-crippling division of labour

[101] 'On the Jewish Question', in T B Bottomore (ed), *Karl Marx: Early Writings*, London 1963 p39 (translated as 'Objectification is the practice of alienation'), in Guddat and Easton, *op cit* (footnote 6), p248 (translated as 'Selling is the practice of externalisation')

[102] *The German Ideology*, London 1965, p43

which made Adam Ferguson say of the English of the eighteenth century: 'We make a nation of helots, and have no free citizens.'[103] A certain degree of specialization is a historic prerequisite for individual development. True enough, the contemporary bourgeois is interested in division of labour only as a means 'of producing more commodities with a given quantity of labour, and, consequently, of cheapening commodities and hurrying on the accumulation of capital'.[104] But in antiquity the division of labour meant something entirely different. 'In most striking contrast with this accentuation of quantity and exchange-value, is the attitude of the writers of classical antiquity, who hold exclusively by quality and use-value. In consequence of the separation of the social branches of production, commodities are better made, the various bents and talents of men select a suitable field, and without some restraint no important results can be obtained anywhere. Hence both product and producer are improved by division of labour.'[105] In support of this argument Marx quoted many ancient authorities, beginning with the author of the *Odyssey*: 'Divers men take delight in divers deeds.'[106] Under the ancient form of division of labour, the qualitative and the quantitative were relatively commensurable: human activities and abilities were not yet subordinated to the abstract-quantitative principle of accumulating capital. This alone helps to explain the high degree of development attained by ancient art. But this is not all.

In ancient society the personality had already begun to emancipate itself from communal ties, but this is not yet the individual of mature commodity economy. 'Collectivism' and the personality had not yet parted company to the extent observed in bourgeois society, where the various form of social relations are, as far as the individual is concerned, 'a mere means to his private ends, an outward

[103] Quoted in *Capital*, I, Moscow 1959, p354
[104] *Capital*, I, Moscow 1959, pp364-365
[105] *ibid*, p365
[106] Quoted in *ibid*, p365 fn 2

necessity'.[107] On the other hand, the de-personalizing effect of the mechanism of capitalist society had not yet developed sufficiently 'to transform man into a hat'. It is true that Greek society depended upon slavery. But would a free citizen of the ancient republic be able to understand how 'the most powerful instrument for shortening labour-time becomes the most unfailing means for placing every moment of the labourer's time and that of his family, at the disposal of the capitalist, for the purpose of expanding the value of his capital',[108] while the labourer himself becomes but a cog in the wheel? The heathens 'understood nothing of political economy and Christianity. They did not, for example, comprehend that machinery is the surest means of lengthening the working day. They perhaps excused the slavery of one on the ground that it was a means to the full development of another. But to preach slavery of the masses, in order that a few crude and half-educated parvenus might become "eminent spinners", "extensive sausage-makers", and "influential shoe-black dealers," to do this, they lacked the bump of Christianity.'[109]

These reflections upon the ancient world show that the historical analogies permeating the workers of 1841-42 remained with the mature Marx. Antiquity and the 'Christian world' (or the world of 'contemporary nations') represented an antithesis which Marx inherited from classical philosophy and aesthetics, and he never renounced this inheritance. Marx's attitude towards the Greeks—those 'normal children' of mankind—also explains his opinion of ancient art which, in contrast to modern art, he considered 'the standard and model beyond attainment'.[110] This also explains Marx's personal admiration for such titans of ancient poetry as Aeschylus.

[107] *A Contribution to the Critique of Political Economy*, London 1971, p188
[108] *Capital*, I, Moscow 1959, p408
[109] *ibid*, pp408-409
[110] *A Contribution to the Critique of Political Economy*, London 1971, p217

The secret of Greek art lay in its undeveloped mode of exchange, a most simple and even naïve form. The productive organization of ancient society was incomparably simpler and clearer than the 'super-sensuous' realm of our commodity market. The efflorescence of ancient culture was based upon the immediate relations between master and slave. Marx called the ancient state and ancient slavery 'manifest *classical* antagonisms' in contradistinction to the 'sanctimonious *Christian* antagonisms' of the contemporary business world.[111]

To put it more exactly, the economic foundation of ancient culture at its highest point consisted in small-scale peasant agriculture and independent handicrafts. 'Peasant agriculture on a small scale, and the carrying on of independent handicrafts, which together form the basis of the feudal mode of production, and after the dissolution of that system, continue side by side with the capitalist mode, also form the economic foundation of the classical communities at their best, after the primitive form of ownership of land in common had disappeared and before slavery had seized on production in earnest.'[112] This mode of production 'flourishes, lets loose its whole energy, attains its adequate classical form, only where the labourer is the private owner of his own means of labour set in action by himself: the peasant of the land which he cultivates, the artisan of the tool which he handles as a virtuoso.'[113] However, in the first place free petty ownership almost always goes hand in hand with slavery or serfdom. Secondly, this mode of production 'is compatible only with a system of production, and a society, moving within narrow and more or less primitive bounds. To perpetuate it would be, as Pecqueur rightly says, "to decree universal medi-

---

[111] 'Critical Notes on "The King of Prussia and Social Reform" ' (1844), in Easton and Guddat (eds), *op cit* (footnote 6), p349

[112] *Capital*, I, Moscow 1959, p334 fn 3

[113] *ibid*, p761

ocrity".[114] The classical mode of small-scale production, in so far as it tended to prevent the development of productive forces, could not help but give way to the concentration of property and the socialization of labour, even if the change had to be wrought by means of 'progress over skulls'. The decline of ancient society, together with its art, was a necessary and progressive phenomenon. 'Then, whatever bitterness the spectacle of the crumbling of an ancient world may have for our personal feelings,' says Marx, 'we have the right, in point of history, to exclaim with Goethe:

> *Sollte diese Qual uns quälen*
> *Da sie unsere Lust vermehrt,*
> *Hat nicht myriaden Seelen*
> *Timurs Herrschaft aufgezehrt?'*[115]

A far more protracted, violent and difficult process of development separates small-scale independent production from the collective production of socialist society. The relative proportionality of the simple economy of undeveloped production gives way to the gigantic disproportions and antagonisms of growing capitalism. The concentration of property in the hands of the few and the 'fearful and painful expropriation of the masses' constitutes the prelude to the history of capital, 'under the stimulus of passions the most infamous, the most sordid, the pettiest, the most meanly odious'.[116] In consequence, all patriarchal relations, and all personal family and communal ties disintegrate, and in their place appears one strong bond—that of 'callous "cash payment".'

[114] *ibid*, p762
[115] 'The British Rule in India', in Marx-Engels, *On Britain*, Moscow 1962, p398

Since they thus have swelled our joy,
Should such torments grieve us then?
Does not Timur's rule destroy,
Myriad souls of living men?

[116] *Capital*, I, Moscow 1959, p762

In *The German Ideology* Marx and Engels call the productive forces of capitalist society destructive in so far as the masses are concerned. Machinery and money, in capitalist society, are examples of such *destructive* forces. 'Money itself is a commodity, an external object, capable of becoming the private property of any individual. Thus social power becomes the private power of private persons. The ancients therefore denounced money as subversive of the economical and moral order of things.'[117]

> ... *Of evils current upon earth,*
> *The worst is money. Money 'tis that sacks*
> *Cities, and drives men forth from hearth and home:*
> *Warps and seduces native innocence,*
> *And breeds a habit of dishonesty.*[118]

In money, 'the radical leveller', all qualitative differences are extinguished. Quality, form, individuality—all these are subordinated to an impersonal quantitative force. Shakespeare knew better than our theorizing bourgeois that money, as the most general form of property, has little in common with personality, that they are utterly contradictory:

> *Gold! Yellow, glittering, precious gold! ...*
> *Thus much of this will make black, white; foul, fair;*
> *Wrong, right; base, noble; old, young; coward,*
> *valiant.*
> *... What this, you gods? Why this*
> *Will lug your priests and servants from your sides,*
> *Pluck stout men's pillows from below their heads.*
> *This yellow slave*
> *Will knit and break religions; bless the accurs'd;*
> *Make the hoar leprosy ador'd; place thieves,*
> *And give them title, knee, and approbation,*
> *With senators on the bench; this is it,*
> *That makes the wappen'd widow wed again.*

[117] *ibid*, p132
[118] *ibid*, p132 fn 3 (quoted in Greek)

> *. . . Come damned earth,*
> *Thou common whore of mankind.*[119]

'The conception of Nature which prevails under the rule of private property and of money is the practical degradation of Nature . . . contempt for theory, for art, for history, for man . . . is the real conscious standpoint and virtue of the monied man.'[120]

This peculiarity of bourgeois society—contempt for aesthetic appreciation—is rooted in the very nature of the mercantile world. 'Born leveller and cynic, it is always ready to exchange not only soul, but body, with any and every commodity, be the same more repulsive than Maritornes herself.'[121] The moral and aesthetic indifference of the commodity as an exchange value was expressed in the utterance of the old Barbon quoted by Marx in *Capital*: 'One sort of wares is as good as another, if the values be equal. There is no difference or distinction in things of equal value.'[122] 'The exchange value of a palace can be expressed in a certain number of boxes of shoe-blacking. On the contrary, London manufacturers of shoe-blacking have expressed the exchange value of their many boxes of blacking, in palaces.'[123] Viewed from the standpoint of the objective relations of capitalist society, the greatest work of art is equal to a certain quantity of manure.

The levelling quality of the capitalist mode of production, with its indifference to the individual characteristics of men and things, is in decided contrast to the social relations which existed in past epochs of flourishing art. Exploitation of man by man was originally a relation of personal dependence. The right to command the labour of others was inseparable from the external appearance and

[119] Shakespeare, *Timon of Athens*, quoted in *ibid*, p132 fn 2
[120] 'On the Jewish Question', in T B Bottomore (ed), *Karl Marx: Early Writings*, London 1963, p37
[121] *Capital*, I, Moscow 1959, p85
[122] *ibid*, p37
[123] *A Contribution to the Critique of Political Economy*, London 1971, p28

D

individual traits of the possessor of this right. Even his bearing, his manner of speech, his clothes, and precious belongings, were attributes of might. Hence, a procession of Lorenzo de' Medici, or a feast in the house of a Greek prince, could be a fitting theme for an artist or a poet. But the economy of capitalist society cannot be described in verse, as the economy of ancient society was described by Hesiod. Personal dependence has been replaced by an abstract, though no less real and cruel, dependence. 'In bourgeois society capital is independent and has individuality, while the living person is dependent and has no individuality.'[124] However, in a sense the capitalist, too, is impersonal, being a mere 'personification' of capital.

[124] *Manifesto of the Communist Party,* in *Selected Works* (2 vol edition), I, p48

13

Whereas ancient society was concerned with the specific quality of a thing, its use-value, the capitalist world is dominated by quantity, exchange-value. Qualitative differences are reduced to simple quantitative relations. The 'degradation of nature' to which Marx referred in working on his Dissertation, he had explained rationally. But much of what was merely hinted at in Marx's earlier works was further developed and translated into materialistic terminology in his works on economics.

While working on the *Critique of Political Economy*, Marx once again returned to problems of art, having been asked by Charles Dana to write an article on aesthetics for the *New American Encyclopaedia*. As Dana proposed to devote only one page to the subject, the request seemed ludicrous to Marx; but nevertheless, lengthy excerpts from various articles on aesthetics in French and German encyclopaedias indicate that he seriously considered the suggestion. The same notebook (1857-58) which contains passages from Meyer's *Konversations-Lexicon* also contains a detailed synopsis of Friedrich Theodor Vischer's famous *Aesthetik*.

Many of the excerpts from Vischer deal with the problem of the interrelation between the nature of things and their aesthetic significance. The latter is by no means a quality inherent in things. In substance there is not a trace of what is called beauty. 'The beautiful exists only for consciousness', paraphrased Marx. 'Beauty is necessary in order that the spectator may merge with it.' Hence beauty is a property of man even though it seems to be a property of things, of 'the beautiful in nature'. This does not mean, however, that the 'aesthetic' is purely subjective. Knowing the role which the subjective-objective productive activity of man plays in Marx's economic and philosophical views, it is easy to grasp the significance of the following passage from Schiller, quoted by Vischer: 'Beauty is simultaneously an object, and a subjective state. It is at once form, when we judge it, and also life, when we feel it. It is at once our state of being and our creation.'

Like the excerpts of the Bonn period, these passages from Vischer reveal a definite tendency to criticize crude naturalism in so far as it mistakes the human for the material and vice versa. This attitude on the part of Marx toward aesthetic values is clearly related to his discovery of commodity fetishism, as well as to his solution of the problem of the subjective and the objective in economic life. Just as in his preparatory studies to the treatise on Christian art, he was here not so much interested in Vischer's interpretation of the 'aesthetic' as he was in its very opposite. But whereas in 1841-42 his criticism of fetishism as inimical to art constituted a democratic negation of the 'old order', while working on *Capital* Marx was interested in categories and forms bordering on the aesthetic because of their analogy to the contradictory vicissitudes of the categories of capitalist economy. The connection between Marx's aesthetic and economic interests is apparent from those passages where he speaks of the 'sublime'; he notes those things which indicate its quantitative character (in the sublime, too, 'the qualitative becomes quantitative'): the tendency toward endless movement, the pursuits of the grandiose, the transcendence of all boundaries and all 'measure'.

Marx's interest in the 'sublime' was by no means accidental. Already in his preparatory studies for his Dissertation he had spoken of the 'dialectics of measure', followed by the reign of 'measurelessness', contradiction and 'discord'. The concept of the measureless received a more concrete interpretation in his 'Economic and Philosophical Manuscripts' (1844). 'The need for money,' wrote Marx, 'is the only genuine need created by political economy. The *quantity* of money becomes more and more man's sole *essential* trait; just as it has reduced everything to an abstraction, so now in its own development it is reduced to a *quantitative* thing. *Measurelessness* and *immeasurability* become its real measure.'[125] In *The Poverty of Philosophy* and in *Capital,* the 'dialectics of measure' is given more developed and scientific form. The relative harmony of simple commodity economy, the birthplace of capitalism, is 'measure'; while capitalism, with its disproportions and contradictions between the ancient methods of appropriation and the higher forms of production, is the violation of 'measure'. Capitalist society is dominated by 'the measureless as measure', as Hegel expressed it.

Measureless is the tendency to amass capital—such is modern 'chrematistics' as opposed to ancient 'oeconomy' [Aristotle]. Measureless and disproportional is capitalistic progress in its very essence: 'production for production's sake.' The contradictory nature of the development of its productive forces is clearly inimical to some fields of spiritual activity—art, for instance. Marx speaks of this in his *Theories of Surplus Value* with a clearness barring all misinterpretation. Spiritual production, wrote Marx, calls for a different kind of labour than that used in material production. The investigation of the connection between given varieties of production and their interrelations 'can get beyond mere empty phrases only when material production is considered *sub sua propia specie*'. 'The form of intellectual production corresponding to capitalism differs from that corresponding to the medieval mode of production. . . . When Storch regards material production from other than the historical point of view, when he regards it as production of material goods in general rather than as a determined, historically-developed and specific form

[125] 'Economic and Philosophical Manuscripts', in T B Bottomore (ed), *Karl Marx: Early Writings*, London 1963, p168

of this production, he removes from under himself the very ground which alone provides an understanding of the ideological components of the ruling classes, and of the free [or "subtle"?] spiritual production of this given social formation. He is unable to rise beyond worthless commonplaces, and these relations are by no means as simple as he imagines. For example, *capitalist production is hostile to certain branches of spiritual production, such as art and poetry* [italics ML]. Unless one understands this, one is liable to find himself under the delusion, so beautifully ridiculed by Lessing, of the French of the eighteenth century: Inasmuch as we have so far surpassed the ancients in mechanics, etc. why not also create an epic poem? And so we got the *Henriade* in place of the *Iliad*!'[126]

Marx subjected to severe criticism all 'general, superficial analogies and comparisons between intellectual and material production'. He ridiculed every attempt to represent artists, men of letters and economists as 'productive workers in Smith's sense' because they allegedly produce 'not simply products *sui generis,* but products of material labour and, therefore, directly, wealth'. All these attempts show that 'even the highest forms of spiritual production are recognized and forgiven by the bourgeoisie only because they [artists, men of letters, etc.] are represented and falsely labelled as direct producers of material wealth.'[127]

In this latter passage Marx expressed very clearly his opinion of the position of art in capitalist society. But what was his conclusion? Did he seek to re-establish the social relations of antiquity, in the mood of the democratic ideals of the Jacobins? Did he issue a call to return to the lost harmony of past ages, as the romantic writers did, as Proudhon did? Quite the contrary. The greatest significance of Marxist theory lies precisely in that it goes beyond the contradiction between the defence of capitalist progress and romanticism. Marx understood that the *destructive* forces of capitalism are at the same time great *productive*

126 *Theories of Surplus Value*, I, London 1969, p285
127 *ibid*, pp286-287

forces. From the very beginning of their development, the progressive elements of capitalism were considered *'le mauvais côté* [the bad side] of society' (*Poverty of Philosophy*). But private interest, which at first is 'an individual crime' against society, turns out to be a source of new, incomparably higher social ties. Social forms of production develop through contradiction, through their very opposite —atomization and separation. Poverty, 'Herodian slaughter of the innocents', extinction of entire peoples, and a great deal more—this is the price which humanity has to pay for the colossal achievements of capitalism: socialization of labour and concentration of production.

'The bourgeois period of history has to create the material basis of the new world—on the one hand universal intercourse founded upon the mutual dependency of mankind, and the means of that intercourse; on the other hand the development of the productive powers of man and the transformation of material production into a scientific domination of natural agencies. Bourgeois industry and commerce creates these material conditions of a new world in the same way as geological revolutions have created the surface of the earth. When a great social revolution shall have mastered the results of the bourgeois epoch, the market of the world and the modern powers of production, and subjected them to the common control of the most advanced peoples, then only will human progress cease to resemble the Hindoo pagan idol, who would not drink the nectar but from the skulls of the slain.'[128]

Thus the positive and the negative, progress and regress, are closely interconnected in the historical growth of humanity.

This general dialectical conception of history naturally determined Marx's views on the development of art. Decadence of artistic creation is inseparable from the progress of bourgeois civilization; on the other hand, the high artistic achievement of past epochs was due to immaturity

[128] 'The Future Results of British Rule in India', in Marx-Engels, *On Britain*, Moscow 1962, pp405-406

of social contradictions. Compare, for instance, medieval craftsmanship with modern industry. 'Among the craftsmen of the middle ages,' wrote Marx, 'there is still to be observed a certain interest in their particular work and in their skill, which was capable of rising to some degree of artistry. But it was also for this reason that every medieval craftsman entered wholly into his work; he had an affectionate, servile attitude towards it, and was dominated by it much more than the modern worker, who is indifferent to his work.'[129] The hired labourer under capitalism can have no interest in his work; nor any aesthetic relation to the product of his labour; this constitutes a progressive phenomenon, in the precise and profound sense of the term.

'Let us consider wages from their most objectionable angle: that my activity is a commodity and that I myself am completely saleable. . . . All patriarchal relations have disappeared, for bargaining, purchase and sale are the only bonds between men, and monetary transactions are the only relationships between employer and worker. . . . Similarly, all the so-called higher forms of labour—intellectual, artistic, etc.—have been transformed into commodities and have thus lost their former sacredness. What tremendous progress to have the whole regiment of clergymen, doctors, lawyers, etc. (and hence religion, law, etc.), defined still more in terms of their commercial value!'[130]

Thus, the very 'contempt for art' so intrinsically characteristic of bourgeois society becomes a mighty revolutionizing factor. Though the bourgeoisie destroys all 'patriarchal, idyllic relations'; though it prostitutes everything, having resolved personal worth into mere exchange value; though it 'has stripped of its halo every occupation hitherto honoured and looked up to with reverent awe',[131] including the work of the poet—nevertheless, and for this

---

[129] *The German Ideology*, London 1965, p67

[130] *Arbeitslohn* (Wages), MEGA, I, 6, pp471-472

[131] *Manifesto of the Communist Party*, in *Selected Works* (2 vol. edition), I, 36

very reason, the 'nihilism' of the bourgeois mode of production is at the same time its greatest historical merit. 'All that is holy is profaned, and man is at last compelled to face with sober senses his real conditions of life and his relations with his kind.'[132] It is necessary and progressive to break illusions and to pitilessly tear asunder the 'motley ties' that bind man to the old social forms. Such is the necessary condition for establishing a truly universal human culture. Already in capitalist society, 'in place of the old local and national seclusion and self-sufficiency, we have intercourse in every direction, universal interdependence of nations. And as in material, so also in intellectual production. The intellectual creations of individual nations become common property. National one-sidedness and narrow-mindedness become more and more impossible, and from the numerous national and local literatures there arises a world literature.'[133]

Hence, paradoxical as this may seem, *the decline of art in capitalist society is progressive even from the standpoint of art itself.*

Marx's doctrine of the disproportional development of artistic culture in relation to society as a whole is closely linked with his theory of social revolution. The disparity between artistic and general social progress is by no means the only contradiction of bourgeois civilization: a deeper, broader contradiction underlies it—that between private profit, preserved since the days of small-scale production, and the social production generated by capitalism. The flourishing art of the past was due to the relative 'proportionment' of the classical mode of production. The antagonisms of bourgeois society naturally arising out of this proportionment resulted in the degradation of art as a special form of culture. But the communist revolution of the working class lays the necessary basis for a new renaissance of the arts on a much broader and higher basis. Marx's conception of this historical dialectic is expressed

[132] *ibid*, p37
[133] *ibid*, p38

in a most remarkable speech delivered on the occasion of the anniversary of the *People's Paper* (April 14, 1856):

'There is one great fact characteristic of this our nineteenth century, a fact which no party dares deny. On the one hand there have started into life industrial and scientific forces which no epoch of the former human history had ever suspected. On the other hand there exist symptoms of decay, far surpassing the horrors recorded of the latter times of the Roman Empire. In our days, everything seems pregnant with its contrary. Machinery, gifted with the wonderful power of shortening and fructifying human labour, we behold starving and over-working it. The newfangled sources of wealth, by some strange, weird spell, are turned into sources of want. The victories of art seem bought by the loss of character. At the same pace that mankind masters nature, man seems to become enslaved to other men or to his own infamy. Even the pure life of science seems unable to shine but on the dark background of ignorance. All our invention and progress seem to result in endowing material forces with intellectual life, and in stultifying human life into a material force. This antagonism between modern industry and science, on the one hand, and modern misery and dissolution, on the other; this antagonism between the productive forces and the social relations of our epoch is a fact, palpable, overwhelming, and not to be controverted. Some may wail over it; others may wish to get rid of modern arts, in order to get rid of modern conflicts. Or they may imagine that so signal a progress in industry wants to be completed by as signal a regress in politics. For our part, we do not mistake the shape of the shrewd spirit that continues to mark all these contradictions. We know that if the newfangled forces of society are to work satisfactorily, they need only be mastered by newfangled men—and such are the working men.'[134]

The contrast between the actual position of art

---

[134] 'Speech on the Anniversary of the *People's Paper*', in Marx-Engels, *On Britain*, Moscow 1962, pp466-467

under capitalism and the enormous possibilities opened up for art by the development of the productive powers of society is merely one instance of the general social contradictions of 'the bourgeois period of history'. The future of art and literature is closely bound up with the solution of these contradictions—which solution cannot be expected, of course, to drop from heaven. The materialist conception of the history of art has nothing in common with the doctrine of the inevitable death of artistic creation. All seemingly 'fatal contradictions' men themselves can solve by a revolutionary and critical construction of the world. But this requires 'newfangled men', as Marx put it—'the working men'. Only struggle can show whether humanity will overcome the contradiction between its artistic and its economic development. And this struggle is, at the moment, merely one aspect of the class struggle of the proletariat, one aspect of the war between two systems, capitalist and socialist. The problem of the future history of art is no abstract question—it is a problem permeated with the socialist world outlook of the proletariat.

Just as Goethe compared the history of humanity to a fugue, the voices of the various nations following one upon another, so Marx might have described the 'voices' of the various social classes representing definite historical modes of production. 'The history of all hitherto existing society is the history of class struggles.' This statement from the *Communist Manifesto* the founders of Marxism knew how to apply with remarkable historical insight, yet without any schematism, to the history of spiritual culture. We already know Marx's attitude towards ancient art, which developed on the basis of a slaveholders' democracy. Because the plight of the hired worker in bourgeois society is the worst kind of slavery—as had been demonstrated by Nicholas Linguet, an eighteenth-century writer whom Marx considered a genius—Marx and Engels, irreconcilably opposed to any defence of capitalism, were always ready to manifest their respect for ancient culture and their disapproval of sentimental criticism of slavery, which implies approbation of the so-called 'free' labour of the capitalist factory. Hence it is obvious why Engels wrote: 'It was slavery that first made possible the division of labour between agriculture and industry on a considerable scale, and along with this, the flower of the ancient world, Hellenism. Without slavery, no Greek state, no Greek art and science; without slavery, no Roman Empire. But without Hellenism and the Roman Empire as a basis, also no modern Europe. We should never forget that our whole economic, political and intellectual development has as its presupposition a state of things in which slavery was as necessary as it was universally recognized. In this sense we are entitled to say: Without the slavery of antiquity, no modern socialism.'[135]

In class society art and culture inevitably acquire a class character. However, the various dominant classes have not played parallel roles in either the general development of culture or in its separate aspects. 'Whereas the decline of former classes—such as the knights, for instance—could furnish material for magnificent tragic works of art, the petty bourgeoisie naturally provides nothing but weak manifestations of fanatical malice, nothing but collections of Sancho Panzian sayings and maxims.'[136] The ideology of the ruling class has always been the prevalent ideology; but, as Marx and Engels repeatedly pointed out, each dominant ideology has its specific hue from which follow virtually automatically this or that intensity and direction of cultural development. Here is a characteristic example: 'There is no doubt that the duel in itself is irrational and the relic of a past stage of culture. At the same time the result of the one-sidedness of *bourgeois* society is that certain individualistic feudal forms assert their rights in opposition to it. The most striking proof of this is to be

[135] Friedrich Engels, *Anti-Dühring*, Part II, Chap 4, Moscow 1969, p216

[136] Marx and Engels, review of G F Daumer, *Die Religion des neuen Weltalters*, in *Aus dem Literarischen Nachlass*, III, *op cit* (footnote 47), p404

found in the civil right of duelling in the United States of America.'[137]

Nevertheless Marx tirelessly stressed the revolutionary role of the bourgeoisie, in an entirely different field, of course. The representatives of feudal land ownership, he wrote in one of the notebooks of 1844, described their opponent, the bourgeois, as a 'sly, prostituted, meddling, deceitful, greedy, venal, heartless, soulless, seditious, antisocial, usurious, pandering, slavish, flattering, opportunistic, swindling, prosaic, competitive and hence pauperizing scoundrel. . . .'[138] On the other hand the bourgeois points out the 'miracle of industry' accomplished in the new capitalistic epoch. 'He characterizes his opponent as an *unenlightened moron* who prefers crude amoral force and serfdom to moral capital and free trade.' He banishes 'his memories, his poetry, his fantasies' by means of 'sarcastic enumeration of all the baseness, cruelty, arrogance, prostitution, infamy, anarchy and rebellion brewed in romantic castles.'[139]

'The bourgeoisie has disclosed how it came to pass that the brutal display of vigour in the Middle Ages, which reactionaries so much admire, found its fitting complement in the most slothful indolence. It has been the first to show what man's activity can bring about. It has accomplished wonders far surpassing Egyptian pyramids, Roman aqueducts, and Gothic cathedrals; it has conducted expeditions that put in the shade all former migrations of nations and crusades.'[140] This high estimation of the role of the bourgeoisie is by no means inconsistent with Marx's contempt for bourgeois commerciality and the prostitution of art. Rather *the inconsistency lies in the very class rule of*

[137] Marx, letter to Lassalle, in *Selected Correspondence*, edited by Dona Torr, London 1934, p111
[138] 'Economic and Philosophical Manuscripts', in T B Bottomore (ed), *Karl Marx: Early Writings*, London 1963, p141
[139] *ibid*, p142
[140] *Manifesto of the Communist Party*, in *Selected Works* (2 vol. edition), I, p37

the bourgeoisie: bourgeois society creates enormous material wealth and powerful means for cultural development, only to demonstrate most vividly its inability to use these means, the limitations of cultural development in a society based upon the exploitation of man by man.

Under the rule of the bourgeoisie, a historically-conditioned (and hence transitory) contradiction between the development of the productive forces of society and its artistic achievement, between technology and art, between science and poetry, between tremendous cultural possibilities and meagre spiritual life, reaches its culmination. In assuming the role of grave-diggers for the bourgeoisie, the proletariat, with every step of the class struggle, brings closer the abolition of the contradictions inherited from all past history. By stripping the propertied classes of all their political and economic advantages, the working class abolishes the division of society into oppressors and oppressed and lays the foundation for destroying the antagonism between town and country and between physical and spiritual labour.

In the process of creating a new society, the proletariat also resolves the contradictions of the cultural development of mankind. Here its historical task is the same as in the sphere of material production. By means of the class struggle it shows the way to a classless culture; by means of the development of an art inspired by the broad and profound worldview of the proletariat, it leads to the abolition of the disparity between social and artistic development, and hence to an unprecedented growth of art upon a wide mass basis. This is the ultimate meaning of all of Marx's comments upon literature and art; this is his historical bequest.

Attempts to interpret Marx's observations concerning the unequal development of art as accidental remarks, or as his 'personal' opinion, ignore the very revolutionary essence of Marxism. One might just as well discard his evaluation of the bourgeois family, bourgeois morality, bourgeois democracy, etc. Nevertheless, this is the manner of bourgeois theoreticians who distinguish between the 'scientific' in Marxism and its 'subjective evaluation' of reality.

The revolutionary materialist dialectics of Marx and Lenin is grounded not only in the doctrine of the unity of all aspects of social life, but also in the acknowledgement of their contradictory relationship and development. Marx loved the art of ancient nations such as Greece. But he was opposed to pseudo-classicism. In fact he predicated the transition from revolutionary democracy to communism upon a conscious realization of the Jacobin mistake—the attempt to restore ancient relations under bourgeois economy (cf *The Holy Family*). In the *Eighteenth Brumaire* he declared that the proletarian revolution cannot even begin so long as such illusions persist. On the other hand the founders of Marxism have nothing in common with apologists of capitalistic progress such as Julian Schmidt, who extolled the factory system and the business character of bourgeois society and ridiculed the admirers of classical antiquity—Goethe and Schiller. Did Marx deplore the high development of art in the past? Did he rejoice at its decline? Neither. Every transition to higher, more developed forms is accompanied by a *negation;* the realization of this destructive side of progress accounts for what may seem like pessimism in Marx's comments upon Greek art. But the dialectics of historical development does not net a negative result. Out of the contradictions and struggle a new, more advanced form of social relations appears. History manifests not only 'disappearance', but also 'the disappearance of the disappearance', as Hegel said. There can be no doubt that Marx's view of the historical destiny of art was essentially optimistic. It was a broad dialectical view of that which takes place in time, that which catches a glimpse of the irresistible advance of the 'shrewd spirit' of world history amidst the miseries and conflicts of the civilized era. 'In the signs that bewilder the middle class, the aristocracy, and the poor prophets of regression, we recognize our old friend Robin Goodfellow, the old mole that can work in the earth so fast, that worthy pioneer—the revolution.'[141]

This is particularly true today, in the critical era of the capitalistic system, when the 'signs' of which Marx spoke in the fifties of the last century are repeated with thousandfold strength. The modern 'prophets of regression', of the Spengler type, render a notable service to the imperialistic bourgeoisie by presenting the post-war crisis of the capitalist system as a collapse of culture in general. Under these modern conditions it is therefore particularly important to point out emphatically that in Marx's aesthetic views there was not a trace of that imaginary 'tragedy of art' which the fascistic professors so love to dwell upon. On the other hand Marx's standpoint had nothing in common with the liberal-positivistic dogma of straight and uniform progress now being attacked by the new prophets of imperialism. Marx's philosophical and aesthetic worldview was dialectical materialism, the broadest and richest doctrine of the development of material activity and spiritual culture.

It is possible now to comprehend that comparison of human history to individual life which we encounter in the introduction to the *Critique of Political Economy*. Here Marx wrote as follows: '. . . The difficulty is not in grasping the idea that Greek art and epos are bound up with certain forms of social development. It rather lies in understanding why they still constitute with us a source of aesthetic enjoyment and in certain respects prevail as the standard and model beyond attainment.

'A man can not become a child again unless he becomes childish. But does he not enjoy the artless ways of the child and must he not strive to reproduce his truth on a higher plane? Is not the character of every epoch revived perfectly true to nature in child nature? Why should the social childhood of mankind, where it had obtained its most beautiful development, not exert an eternal charm as an

[141] 'Speech on the Anniversary of the *People's Paper*', in Marx-Engels, *On Britain*, Moscow 1962, p467

age that will never return? There are ill-bred children and precocious children. Many of the ancient nations belong to the latter class. The Greeks were normal children. The charm their art has for us does not conflict with the primitive character of the social order from which it had sprung. It is rather the product of the latter, and is rather due to the fact that the unripe social conditions under which the art arose and under which alone it could appear can never return.'[142]

This comparison of 'the artistic period' of history to the childhood and youth of human society has a long history of its own. It is to be found, in dozens of variations, in all kinds of writers, from Plato to Hölderlin, from imaginative mystics of the thirteenth century to some bourgeois writers of our own day. As to Marx himself, it was nothing more than a figurative comparison inherited from classical German philosophy. Hegel gave it a prominent role. In his lectures on the philosophy of history, he summarized his interpretation of the progress of development in the form of two basic 'categories of Spirit'. Everything that exists loses its freshness and is subject to *disappearance*. But the process of development does not stop at this point. There comes a *return of youth—die Verjüngung*—on a new and higher level. It is interesting to note, however, that Hegel did not remain consistent in his own scheme of development. He described the Oriental world as the childhood, the Greek world as the youth, the Roman world as the maturity, and the Christian-German world as the old age of the Universal Spirit. It would seem that this scheme demands continuation; that at a certain stage of its development the 'ageing world' must give way to a new 'youth', a new social form, a new cycle of historical development. But the specific character of Hegel's philosophy of history consisted precisely in that he was forced to abandon his dialectical method and to conclude the process with the period of old age, that is, with contemporary bourgeois

[142] *A Contribution to the Critique of Political Economy*, London 1971, p217

society. 'The Old Age of *Nature* is weakness,' wrote Hegel, 'but that of *Spirit* is its perfect maturity and *strength*.'[143] The historical path of the nations is ended; all that remains for us is to comprehend the past.

This doctrine was subjected to criticism already at the time of the disintegration of the Hegelian school. Before the radical Hegelians stood the 'problem of the future' as well as the problem of the revolution. But a real demonstration of the transition from the 'pre-history of human society' to a new and higher form of society was given only by Marxism. Consequently we may say quite justifiably that historical materialism restored to the category of *Verjüngung* that meaning which Hegel withheld from it.

How are we to reconcile the doctrine of the efflorescence of culture under communist society with the passage just quoted from the introduction to the *Critique of Political Economy*? Does not this passage acknowledge that a rebirth of art is impossible? Such inferences have often been made, but they are false. The manuscript of the introduction breaks off, unfortunately, at the point where, following the description of the unconditional decline of Greek art, there should begin the demonstration of a possible new efflorescence of art. In Marx's outline there is one phrase, however, which proves how little his historical views resembled an elegy. Must not a man, asked Marx, 'strive to reproduce his truth (*seine Wahrheit zu reproduzieren*) on a higher plane?' This question is the key to Marx's real thought. The concept of reproduction (*Reproduktion*) played an important role in all German philosophy, including Hegel. In the *Science of Logic* and elsewhere, it appears as the life process of reproduction of the species. I reproduce my truth in my child; thus the negation contained within my own life is in its turn negated. Marx, too, applied this concept to human life in the same way. For instance, in his *Critique of Hegel's 'Philosophy of Right'* he wrote as follows: 'The highest

[143] G W F Hegel, *Philosophy of History*, New York 1956, pp108-109

function of the body is sexual activity. The highest constitutional act of a king is his sex act, for in this manner he reproduces the king and perpetuates his own body. The body of his son is the reproduction of his own body, the creation of a royal body.'[144] In *The German Ideology* Marx deciphered the fantastic speculative notion of the 'reproduction of human kind' as the historical process of transition to communism. Many more reasons might be cited to show that Marx's words concerning the reproduction of man's truth is no more than a traditional, metaphorical expression referring to the third and highest step of the dialectical process. Marx never held the doctrine of the ultimate decay of art, despite the naïve imaginations of some of his 'commentators'. This doctrine is a simplified and schematized form of the idealistic dogma of the final decay of art in the kingdom of pure reason, that is in bourgeois society. But since history does not end with bourgeois society, the decadence of art under capitalism is not the last step in the evolution of creative art.

[144] Marx, *Critique of Hegel's 'Philosophy of Right'* (ed. Joseph O'Malley), Cambridge 1970, p40

14

The historical role of the capitalist mode of production is to bring into the sharpest possible focus the contradictions of social progress; at the same time it prepares the ground for the annihilation of all these inequalities and antagonisms. The very division of labour gives rise to contradictions between the three 'elements': 'productive forces', 'social relations', and 'consciousness'. The social division of labour is not, however, an eternal category. As a class stratification of society it disappears, and as a professional hierarchy it withers away in the transition to communist society.

But what does this transition mean with regard to aesthetic creation? Does it not mean the destruction of all distinctions between the aesthetic and the non-aesthetic in art, just as in life the contradiction between the artist and the ordinary mortal is removed? Does not collectivism, generally speaking, suppress all individual originality and talent? Such are some of the bourgeois objections to communism. These objections Marx and Engels dealt with in criticizing Max Stirner's *The Ego and his Own*. Stirner, one of the founders of anarchism, distinguished between 'human' work, which can be organized collectively, and 'individual' work, which cannot be socialized in any manner. For who can take the place of a Mozart or a Raphael?

'Here again, as always,' wrote Marx and Engels, 'Sancho [i.e. Stirner] is out of luck in his choice of practical examples. He thinks that "no one can compose your music in your stead, or execute your designs for a painting.

Raphael's works can be done by no other." But Sancho should have known that not Mozart himself, but someone else, largely composed and completely finished Mozart's *Requiem*, and that Raphael "executed" only a small portion of his frescoes.

'He imagines that the so-called organizers of labour wish to organize the whole activity of every individual, whereas it is precisely they who make a distinction between directly productive labour, which must be organized, and labour which is not directly productive. As far as the latter kind of labour is concerned, they do not think, as Sancho imagines, that everybody can work in Raphael's place, but rather that everybody who has a Raphael in him should be able to develop unhindered. Sancho imagines that Raphael created his paintings independently of the division of labour then existing in Rome. If he will compare Raphael with Leonardo da Vinci and Titian, he will see to what extent the works of art of the first were conditioned by the flourishing of Rome, then under the influence of Florence; how the works of Leonardo were conditioned by the social milieu of Florence, and later those of Titian by the altogether different development of Venice. Raphael, like any other artist, was conditioned by the technical advances made in art before him, by the organization of society and the division of labour in his locality, and finally, by the division of labour in all the countries with which his locality maintained relations. Whether an individual like Raphael is able to develop his talent depends entirely upon demand, which in turn depends upon the division of labour and the consequent educational conditions of men.

'In proclaiming the individual character of scientific and artistic work, Stirner places himself far below the bourgeoisie. Already in our time it has been found necessary to organize this "individual" activity. Horace Vernet would not have had the time to produce one-tenth of his paintings if he had considered them works which "only this individual can accomplish". In Paris the tremendous demand for vaudeville and novels has given rise to an organization of labour for the production of these wares, which are at least better, at any rate, than their "individual" competitors in Germany.'[145] Thus bourgeois society itself makes attempts to organize the higher forms of spiritual labour. 'Needless to say, however, all these organizations based upon the modern division of labour achieve results which are still very inadequate, and represent an advance only by comparison with the short-sighted self-sufficiency existing until now.'[146] But we should not confuse this so-called 'organization of labour' with communism. In communist society those confounded questions concerning the disparity between highly gifted persons and the masses, disappear. 'The exclusive concentration of artistic talent in certain individuals, and its consequent suppression in the broad masses of the people, is an effect of the division of labour. Even if in certain social relations everyone could become an excellent painter, that would not prevent everyone from being also an original painter, so that here too the difference between "human" work and "individual" work becomes a mere absurdity. With a communist organization of society, the artist is not confined by the local and national seclusion which ensues solely from the division of labour, nor is the individual confined to one specific art, so that he becomes exclusively a painter, a sculptor, etc.; these very names express sufficiently the narrowness of his professional development and his dependence on the division of labour. In a communist society, there are no painters, but at most men who, among other things, also paint.'[147]

Collectivism, far from suppressing personal originality, in reality provides the only solid ground for an all-sided development of personality. Marx and Engels stated this emphatically in *The German Ideology*. They knew full well that a new cycle of artistic progress can begin only with the victory of the proletariat, the abolition of private

[145] *The German Ideology*, London 1965, p431
[146] *ibid*
[147] *ibid*, pp431-432

property, the spread of communist relations. Only then can all the forces now exhausted by capitalist oppression be liberated. 'The destruction of private property is the complete assimilation of all human feelings and characteristics.' The new society, wrote Marx, in criticism of 'crude', levelling communism, does not stand for the 'abstract negation of all education and civilization'. It does not propose 'to suppress talent by force'. Quite the contrary, 'in communist society—the only society in which the original and free development of individuals is no mere phrase—this development is contingent precisely upon the very association of individuals, an association based partly on economic premises, partly upon the necessary solidarity of the free development of all, and finally upon the universal activity of individuals in accordance with the available productive forces. Thus the question here concerns individuals on a definite historical level of development, and not any random individuals. . . . Naturally the consciousness of these individuals with respect to their mutual relations is likewise altogether different, and as remote from the "principle of love" or "*dévouement*" as from egoism.'[148]

Communist society removes not only the abstract contradiction between 'work and pleasure' but also the very real contradiction between feeling and reason, between 'the play of bodily and mental powers' and 'the conscious will'. Together with the abolition of classes and the gradual disappearance of the contradiction between physical and spiritual labour, comes that all-sided development of the whole individual which the greatest social thinkers hitherto could only dream about. Only communist society, in which 'the associated producers regulate their interchange with nature rationally, bring it under their common control, instead of being ruled by it as by some blind power', can establish the material basis for 'the development of human power which is its own end, the true realm of freedom'.

[148] *ibid*, pp483-484

'. . . The shortening of the working day is its fundamental premise.'[149]

According to Marx's doctrine, therefore, communism creates conditions for the growth of culture and art compared to which the limited opportunities that the slaves' democracy offers to a privileged few must necessarily seem meagre. *Art is dead! LONG LIVE ART!* this is the slogan of Marx's aesthetics.

[149] *Capital,* III, Moscow 1966, p820

Index

Werner Thönnessen

The Emancipation of Women :

The Rise and Decline of the Women's Movement in Germany 1863-1933

The revival of the women's movement in recent years has generated renewed interest in the origins of the socialist theory of women's emancipation. In this book, Werner Thönnessen shows how this theory developed and how it changed with the fortunes of the working-class movement as a whole.

Developments in Germany over the past century have been of immense importance for socialist theory and practice everywhere. The debate on revisionism at the turn of the century, the failed revolution of 1919, the development of the vast German Communist Party and the collapse of the working-class movement with the advance of fascism have been crucial stages in the rise and temporary decline of the socialist movement. Thönnessen now shows that the development of the women's movement in Germany has been equally important and that a knowledge of its rise and decline up till 1933 is essential if earlier mistakes are not to be repeated.

Thönnessen has gathered a wealth of new material. His conclusion is clear ; the fortunes of the women's movement will rise or decline with the fortunes of the working-class movement as a whole, and any demands that fall short of the liberation of working men and women alike will ultimately remain ineffective.

Born in Saarbrücken in 1929, Werner Thönnessen studied industrial sociology and the history of the labour movement for a PhD at Frankfurt am Main university. He has worked for many years as an administrator for IG Metall, the German metalworkers' union. Now assistant general secretary of the International Metalworkers' Federation, Thönnessen has written many journal articles on trade union subjects.

Translated from the German by Joris de Bres

£1.50 paperback ISBN 0 902818 26 0
£3.75 hardback   ISBN 0 902818 27 9
    192 pages

15p post and packing from
Pluto Press Limited
Unit 10 Spencer Court
7 Chalcot Road
London NW1 8LH

Sheila Rowbotham

Hidden from History:

300 years of women's oppression and the fight against it.

This book is a study of the changing position of women in England from the puritan revolution until the 1930s.

The book is in five parts: work and the family from puritan times to the early 18th century radicalism ; new forms of resistance to changes in oppression and exploitation ; the rise of the feminist movement and the response of trade unions and socialists to it ; the suffragettes and the socialists ; and the decline of the women's (and socialist) movement in the nineteen-twenties and thirties.

Sheila Rowbotham brings together a mass of material on birth control, abortion and female sexuality ; on the complex relationship of women's oppression and class exploitation ; and on the attempts to fuse the struggles against these two.

This book is a product of her involvement in the women's liberation movement. It concludes that feminist socialism is both urgent and possible but it depends on 'our capacity to relate to the working class and the action of working-class women in transforming women's liberation according to their needs'.

Sheila Rowbotham has been active in the socialist movement for ten years. Author of the pamphlet *Women's Liberation and the New Politics,* reprinted in an anthology of women's writings, *The Body Politic,* she has written for *Black Dwarf, Idiot International, Shrew* and *Socialist Worker.* She has contributed to a number of books on women's liberation and written two full-length books: *Women, Resistance and Revolution* and *Women's Consciousness, Man's World* (to be published later this year).

Hidden from History is the first book she has written as a socialist for a socialist publisher.

£1.50 paperback ISBN 0 902818 28 7
£3.30 hardback   ISBN 0 902818 29 5
   192 pages

15p post and packing from

Pluto Press Limited
Unit 10 Spencer Court
7 Chalcot Road
London NW1 8LH
Telephone 01 - 722 0141

Raya Dunayevskaya

Marxism and Freedom

First published in 1958, this internationally-acclaimed work presents Marx's theories as 'the generalization of the instinctive striving of the proletariat for a new social order, a truly human society'. The author, who was secretary to Leon Trotsky during his exile in Mexico, has included a new chapter on the Chinese cultural revolution in this third edition.

£1.25 paperback ISBN 0 902818 50 8
£3.00 hardback ISBN 0 902818 04 X
    378 pages

15p post and packing from
Pluto Press Limited
Unit 10 Spencer Court
7 Chalcot Road
London NW1 8LH
Telephone 01 - 722 0141

Karl Korsch

Three Essays on Marxism

Karl Korsch (1886-1961) author of *Marxism and Philosophy* was an outstanding German theoretician of the revolutionary communist movement. These three essays, 'Leading Principles of Marxism', 'Introduction to Capital' and 'Why I am a Marxist' were written in the 1930s. They represent Korsch's attempt to keep Marxism alive as the theory of the self-emancipation of the working class after the peak of the post-war revolutionary movement had passed.

50p paperback ISBN 0 902818 08 2
£1.25 hardback ISBN 0 902818 07 4
    71 pages

10p post and packing from
Pluto Press Limited
Unit 10 Spencer Court
7 Chalcot Road
London NW1 8LH
Telephone 01 - 722 0141